SUPERNATURAL
SCOTLAND

LILY SEAFIELD

with additional
material by
Rosalind Patrick

LOMOND BOOKS

Published 2005 by Geddes & Grosset, David Dale House, New Lanark, ML11 9DJ for **LOMOND BOOKS**

© 2005 Geddes & Grosset

Main text by Lily Seafield with additional material by Rosalind Patrick.

ISBN 1 84204 079 0

Printed and bound in Poland

contents

introduction

Scotland is famed for her wild and variant landscape, from the high peaks and bleak, endless moors of the Highlands to the low, rolling fields of the Borders, from dense forestry to gleaming lochs, white sands to ruinous, jaggy coves.

She is famous too for her history, the blood-stained hands of her kings and queens, the violent rebellions and valiant underdogs. As she is for her whisky and golf-courses, literature and music, philosophers and economists.

But Scotland has another great claim to fame, and it is this that furnishes us with the subject of our book. No nation on earth is more inundated with reportings of hauntings and paranormal activity, and people travel thousands of miles to visit our ghostliest centres, places like the mysterious vaults buried beneath Edinburgh's Old Town, and the battlefield at Culloden, with its brooding, troubled atmosphere.

Walk along any main town high street where you will see the signs for ghost tours and haunted pub crawls and you will be left in no doubt that our supernatural heritage has become as great a tourist draw as our more traditional charms.

Theories abound as to why Scotland should be such a magnet for otherworldy activity. One prominent one being that the Celtic character is more sensitive than most to what lies beyond, is more intuitive and less earth-bound.

Perhaps this instinct explains why spiritualism and mediumship thrive in modern Scotland, the country that brought forth some its greatest practitioners, including the legendary Helen Duncan, aka Hellish Nell, the last woman to be tried - and convicted - under the 1735 Witchcraft Act. This war-time Physical Medium, celebrated for her seeming ability to make the dead walk amongst the living, is written off as the worst kind of fraudster by some, while hailed as a martyr to her art by others.

Gordon Smith is one of today's most internationally renowned

Spiritualists, credited with some truly remarkable demonstrations. Yet it would be difficult to find anyone more strongly connected to his Scottish roots, more grateful for his down-to-earth Glaswegian upbringing and the humour of the city which remains his home.

This Celtic sensitivity, if such it is, is doubtless informed by the landscape, which has the ability, not just to change from one ten mile stretch to the next, but from one moment to the next. You can gaze down from the summit of Ben A'an, in the Lomond mountain range, and see for miles, down onto the still surface of Loch Katrine and out across the peaks, then suddenly find your view obstructed, yourself shrouded in billowing white mist and the day lost to sight. But as you descend, out comes the sun again and the long, lavish views, only to disappear instantaneously beneath a freak shower of hailstones. Like all peoples, we are affected by changes in light and atmospheric pressure, our imaginations are triggered by them, and our senses heightened. Perhaps this is what gave rise to our tales of grey giants treading softly behind travellers in remote places, and curious creatures that suddenly appear by roadsides and shores, and vanish in the blink of an eye.

Perhaps too, this at least partly explains why the witchhunts of the 16th and 17th centuries reached such hysterical proportions in Scotland, where hundreds of innocent men and women were burnt to death by zealots who feared for their newfound religion, Christianity. The horrors of that time have never been completely forgotten. Nor has the ancient, generally benign, belief system that underpinned "the Craft". Today, as secularism continues in its ascendancy, Scotland is witnessing something of a renaissance in pagan rites and Wicca, the modern reconstruction of what remains of the old religions.

The Scottish psyche is also undoubtedly informed by changes in society. The strict doctrine of Presbyterianism and the insistence of rationalism created a hunger for the inexplicable and fantastic. "Plain claes and purridge" leaves little for the imagination to feed on, so it is little wonder the old tales, passed on by word-of-mouth through generations, remained popular even as John Knox railed against superstition and nonsense.

There is also a link with ancient Celtic beliefs, notably that the spirits of the dead remain amongst the living. The neolithic standing stones, burial cairns and mysterious straight tracks that cross-hatch the countryside indicate that here was a society that revered its ancestors and regularly paid homage to them. These spirits guarded the living, and perhaps even guided them.

Earth energy investigators, whose specialism takes in ley lines and sacred sites, believe that the ancients had means of communicating with the dead and that certain places, such as standing stone circles, operated as portals to another dimension.

This finds a modern translation in the science of UFOlogy. Bizarrely, and noone as yet has posited even a credible theory as to why, Scotland clocks up more UFO sightings than anywhere else in the world. And the most popular destination for extra-terrestrial visitors is the unremarkable town of Bonnybridge, in the Central Region.

Could these sightings be related to those ancient portals? Or to the ability of our ancestors, some vestiges of which perhaps survive in people born today, to see through the darkness to the worlds beyond?

the spirit worlð: communing with the ðead

Spiritualism is the art of communing with the dead and where there are those who dismiss it as a Victorian parlour game with special effects, there are others who sincerely believe in it and who cleave to it as a comforting proof of the eternal life of the spirit.

Scotland has a long tradition of Spiritualism. Indeed, some of the most celebrated names associated with Spiritualism hail from, or lived in, Scotland - Arthur Conan Doyle, Helen Duncan, Albert Best and Gordon Smith, to name but four.

To those with faith, Spiritualism is much more than a spooky pastime; in fact, it is a religion and is recognised as such by the British government.

The Seven Principles of Spiritualism, as revealed to Emma Hardinge Britten, a Spiritualist pioneer, do not contradict a belief in a single, all-seeing God, nor the idea of a human soul being brought to account in the hereafter for conduct during Earthly life.

The Principles can be summarised as follows:

1: God is the father of mankind.

2: Humanity is one family; we are all each other's sisters and brothers.

3: Communion with the spirit world is possible and desirable as spirits can offer us guidance and wisdom from the Other Side.

4: The human soul lives on after physical death.

5: We each must take personal responsibility for ourselves and our actions.

6: For our deeds on Earth, whether good or evil, we will receive compensation or retribution in the afterlife.

7: Even after death, the possibility of redemption and spiritual progress is available to every soul.

Spiritualists believe that we are surrounded by spirits, though not everyone has awareness, not even every Spiritualist. Only "sensitive", psychic people can access this parallel universe and even then, only through honing and developing their skills.

These sensitives, who become known as Mediums because they serve as a channel of communication, usually discover their gift in early life, often during adolescence. They may encounter someone who has recently died, or a beloved relative, and have what appears to be a perfectly normal conversation with them.

Or, like Alannah Knight, the Edinburgh crime-writer and psychic, they may have access to the worlds beyond in a more direct way. Roddy Martine, author of Supernatural Scotland, recounts how the 16-year-old Alannah was visiting Holyrood Palace in Edinburgh with her parents, when she suddenly decided to leave the rather serious guided tour and take a stroll outside in the garden. This garden was beautifully ornate and bordered by unspoilt grassy aspects. Modern Edinburgh had curiously vanished. As she walked further into the garden, she came across a freshly dug grave, roughly marked as that of a D. Riccio.

It was not until 30 years later, when she next returned to the capital, that Alannah realised how odd this experience had been. Seeing the High School on Calton Hill, where before she had seen only grazing sheep and a windmill, brought it home to her that the place she had visited before had been another country – the past.

Further investigation led her to believe that she had seen Holyrood Palace as it had been four centuries previously, when Riccio, the ill-fated Italian foreign secretary to Mary, Queen of Scots, had just been brutally stabbed to death and his body flung into a rude grave in the Palace grounds.

Riccio's body, according to a plaque on the wall of Canongate Kirk, was later removed from Holyrood Palace to the nearby church, though no-one has ever been able to pinpoint the exact location of his original grave.

Furthermore, old maps reveal that the layout of Holyrood's immediate environs when Mary was on the throne was, as Alannah had witnessed, an intricate set-up of walled gardens.

All very curious, unless you take on board the words of the

Rev Charles Robertson, of Canongate Kirk, who asserts: "There is no now and then, only now. Time and place belong to the eternal here and now, and we dip in and out of them constantly."

Or rather, those with certain sensitivities can.

Once identified as psychic, people are encouraged to develop their skill in Spiritualist "development circles", where they receive advice and encouragement, and the chance to practise their art in a safe, non-critical environment.

Gordon Smith, also known as the Psychic Barber, lives and works in Glasgow, and was invited to join a Development Circle by several mediums who singled him out as someone possessed of a very special psychic gift.

In the course of these Circle meetings, Gordon learnt, not just how to clear his mind and, as he says in his autobiography *Spirit Messenger*, "wait for the spirit world to draw close to you and 'impress' you with the messages they wished to convey", but also to develop sufficient self-awareness to distinguish between his imagination and his "natural ability to perceive spirit people."

These days, he conducts both public meetings, at which he will convey messages to audience members, and private sittings. In both cases, he transmits messages, in his own voice, that he "hears" from the spirit world, often through the medium of his Spirit Guide. His sessions are reassuringly low-key, often notable for their humour and warmth.

psychic communication

Physical mediums

Not all Spiritualist mediums work in the same way. There are the so-called physical mediums, who are able not just to communicate with spirits, but make them visibly manifest. Helen Duncan, the famous war-time medium and the last woman ever to be tried under the 1735 Witchcraft Act, was a physical medium.

Testimonies to her extraordinary powers include astonishing accounts of human forms rendered visible through ectoplasm emanating from the medium's own body. People looked on in amazement as long-dead loved ones materialised before their very eyes, sometimes perfect and recognisable in every detail.

One or two of these incredible events are even captured on photographs.

Clairaudience

Other mediums operate on a less spectacular level, and often through choice. Albert Best, the Belfast-born medium who made Glasgow his home but travelled the world practising his craft, is said to have told the Spirit World that he "didn't want that".

He, like many before and after him, was a clairaudient. That is, he transmitted the messages he received from the Spirit World, often not understanding the implications or content of these messages but simply passing them on to their intended recipients.

There are other variations of mediumship, such as a clairvoyant, who literally "sees" the spirits and is thus able to describe the appearance of the sender of the message. Some clients find it enormously comforting to know that a loved one who died, for example, wounded in a war or as a result of a disfiguring illness is, in death, restored to their former selves.

Clairsentients

Clairsentients actually "feel" their spirits, experiencing pain or illness just as the departed soul felt them. Horribly, they may even experience how a spirit met their physical end.

Clairomas

Clairomas, as the word suggests, experience smells associated with the communicating spirit; it may be someone's pipe tobacco, or a special perfume.

Automatic writing

Another form of psychic communication is automatic writing. In this case, the medium holds a pen and paper at the ready in order to allow the communicating spirit to convey its message through the medium's hand. The medium, driven by the spirit, scribbles fast and furious messages which, like the spoken ones, are generally only explicable to the intended recipient.

Many mediums combine a number of these elements.

Trance mediums

Finally, there are trance mediums, who appear to be taken over by the voices of spirits which speak through them. This form of mediumship, where odd, sometimes very strange, voices emanate from an apparently sleeping person, has led some to believe that Spiritualism is, in fact, a form of demonic possession.

sceptics

Most mediums are happy to deal with sceptics and agree that, after all, why should you believe something that you have never personally witnessed? They urge people to attend Spiritualist meetings with an open mind. However, there are a number of questions that surface again and again with regards to Spiritualism.

One that is often asked is how can a medium be sure that the spirit with whom they are communicating is not malevolent and bent on imparting destructive messages? One answer is that not every spirit is a good one. Gordon Smith relates a hilarious, though also rather sad, tale of a spirit who wished to communicate with his still living wife.

On hearing that it was her no-good husband, this Glasgow housewife responded: "If he thinks for one bloomin' minute that I have anything to say to him, he's up a bloody gum tree! The day that ratbag died was the happiest of my life!"

Needless to say, the less-than-ideal husband "scuttled (back) to his realm of guilt and remorse."

More seriously, mediums do warn amateurs to beware of evil spirits, who can be called up easily enough, through seances and ouija board sessions, but prove much harder to get rid off. Most mediums have one or more spirit guides, who are there to ensure that "lower" or malevolent spirits do not escape through the portal from the Other Side, created temporarily by the medium during a sitting or trance.

Another question – or rather accusation, – that is raised by sceptics is that mediums make statements that are so general they are bound to apply to someone in a large audience. Couple this with the fact that many mediums cannot always offer a name for a spirit, and it is easy to see the comparison with daily newspaper horoscopes in which readers are given such nebulous information that practically any outcome would fit.

The case for the defence includes Albert Best, a former postman, who was able to deliver not just precise names, but addresses too.

A further charge is that mediums seed their audiences with "plants" so that, even if the real messages prove vague and unconvincing, the psychic can fall back on a couple of sure things. This, the reasoning goes, ensures that audience members go away with the impression that the medium made meaningful contact with the "other side", even if they were not lucky enough to be recipients this time.

There is also the claim that mediums respond to verbal and non-verbal clues unwittingly given by audience members. For example, a young woman twisting a wedding ring could be a new bride experiencing marital problems. Or the medium could say he has a "Dave" and an eager audience member will supply the full name, and even betray details of the relationship with him or her.

There have been studies conducted by, amongst others, the Society for Psychical Research, which was established in 1882 by a group of Cambridge scholars, with the express purpose of investigating paranormal activities in a rigorously scientific manner. Past presidents, including former British Prime Minister AJ Balfour, eminent physician Sir William Crookes and physiologist and Nobel Laureate Charles Richet, testify to the high status of its membership.

One such investigation, published in the Journal of the Society in January 2001 and conducted by Gary E Schwartz, Linda GS Russick, Lonnie A Nelson and Christopher Barentsen, considered the very issues just outlined.

They hoped to ascertain whether a skilled medium really could obtain accurate and replicable information from the spirit world, or whether, indeed, they relied on the information they could glean from their sitters.

Five individual mediums took part, and one subject, unknown to them all. The subject, a woman from Arizona, had experienced six significant losses within the previous decade and prior to the sittings, completed a comprehensive questionnaire detailing the circumstances and nature of her losses. After which, she met with each medium. Needless to say, the mediums were barred from conferring with each other. To eliminate the possibility of visual clues, the woman sat behind a screen during each sitting. And to eliminate the possibility of verbal clues, she was allowed to give only "yes" and "no" answers to any questions the mediums may ask of her.

Video cameras recorded each sitting and full, verbatim transcripts were made.

The results were incredible. The study showed that the mediums achieved an average accuracy of 83 per cent. The average accuracy for 68 control subjects, where chance was the only factor in play, was by contrast only 36 per cent.

In a further experiment conducted by the same team, accuracy levels were recorded at an average of 77 per cent. Leading the researchers to conclude that skilled mediums can indeed obtain accurate and replicable information from the spirit world.

Not everyone is convinced, some maintaining that other, as yet unknown, factors may be at work. And there are, unfortunately, enough fraudulent Mediums at work to make anyone wary.

Whatever your view, there is no doubt that Spiritualism is alive and well in the modern world, particularly in Scotland where Spiritualist churches flourish in major conurbations and small towns alike and where new mediums, such as the now internationally-renowned Gordon Smith, keep springing up, generation after generation.

origins of spiritualism

As far back as 540 BC, Pythagoras was interpreting messages from the dead, assisted by his student Phlolaus. However, it took two millennia for communion with the dead to become a widely practised phenomenon.

Spiritualism exerts an ever-growing fascination in our modern world. It's a curious paradox that, the more we progress in terms of technology, science, philosophy, the more we seem drawn to the inexplicable, to the realms of intuition, other-worldiness and spiritualism.

Perhaps then we should not be surprised that 19th-century Scotland, a nation that brought forth great inventors and thinkers, the pioneers of the Enlightenment, should also have been a nursery for the Spiritualist movement.

Certainly the Victorian era was one of unprecedented change, in which all the old certainties were being swept away by the impatient hand of modernity. Traditional systems of labour were undermined and ultimately made obsolete by the new age of machinery, long-standing communities collapsed as people migrated to the now sprawling cities in search of work, religious tenets were contradicted by scientific breakthroughs, and the ancient and comforting idea of earthly life as a precursor to a heavenly afterlife went up in smoke.

The Foxes

To those who recoiled from the new, seemingly soulless world, the strange tale of the Fox sisters must have been irresistible.

To explain a little of the origins of Spiritualism we must leave the shores of Scotland briefly to look at the events of 19th-century New York State. Margaret and Kate Fox were two young, perfectly normal sisters, growing up in the small town of Hydesville, south of Buffalo, New York. The only extraordinary factor was that the house in which they lived was reputed to be haunted, by the spirit of a travelling salesmen who had been murdered in their cellar many years before. This latter, however, was unknown to them initially, and the town records were a little sketchy.

The girls, then aged 9 and 11 years, were constantly troubled by knocking and banging sounds during the night. So much so that, on the night of 31 March 1848, Kate attempted to communicate with the restless spirit. Urging Mr Splitfoot, as she nicknamed him, to do as she did, she clapped her hands twice. Mr Splitfoot responded with two loud raps. Establishing a system of two raps for yes and one for no, the girls were able to conduct a coherent dialogue with their guest, who told them of his history and led them to a fragment of skull and hair interred in the cellar.

The Fox girls' father called in the neighbours to testify to the veracity of these incredible events and word soon spread. Joined by their sister Leah, the Fox girls were soon embarking on spiritualist tours, where people gathered to witness their terrifying yet intriguing dialogues with the dead, who communicated through loud raps on the table top or by manipulating objects around the room.

It began as a craze, an absolute must-see on a par with freak shows and circuses. But it grew to be much more than that. Naturally, it attracted the ire of the established churches. The Fox sisters, and those who followed in their footsteps, were subject to verbal and physical abuse and were denounced as ungodly and blasphemous.

Yet, by the close of the century, Spiritualism had elevated itself from the status of vaudeville to a serious religion with millions upon millions of followers.

Even more curiously, Margaret Fox, in later life, confessed that the events at Hydesville had all been a hoax. The knocking sounds – she now claimed – had been made by the girls themselves, who were adept at cracking their toes. The whole enterprise had started out as a prank to scare their mother and had simply got out of hand.

Defenders of the Spiritualist faith, however, point out that Margaret, by then a penniless widow and heavy drinker, was coaxed to confess by an enterprising news reporter offering a substantial fee. And in any case, in 1891, she retracted the confession. Furthermore, how else could three unworldly young women have known about the murdered salesmen other than via a supernatural agency?

Spiritualism thrived in the teeth of its detractors and Margaret's confession, perhaps because it fulfilled a very human need – that being to communicate with the dead, and be comforted by the certain knowledge that everything did not end with the death of the body.

The Fox sisters inspired people across America, despite the disapproval of the church. Their home town, which still has a plaque proudly commemorating the events as the "first proof of the continuity of life, which was the beginning of modern

Spiritualism" is a hotbed of Spiritualist activity and something of a pilgrimage destination for modern-day seekers of communion with their dead.

Emma Hardinge Britten and the spirit of Robert Owen

One of the many people inspired by the Foxes was the mother of English-born Emma Hardinge Britten, then living in America. Thus, when the young Emma received an inexplicable message from she knew not where informing her that the ship she was awaiting – *The Pacific* – had gone down at sea, her mother seized on it as proof of a fledgling psychic sensibility. Emma, it seems, did not need too much coaxing and was soon sufficiently skilled in the art of mediumship to give readings to the public, including some in the company of Kate Fox.

Emma is perhaps most famous for being the recipient, in 1871, of the Seven Principles, which were she received in a message from the spirit of Robert Owen (1771–1858), the great Welsh-born social reformer, best known for establishing the model village of New Lanark, in Scotland, to function along the lines of socialism. These Seven Principles became the foundation stone of the Spiritualist religion and are still adhered to today.

Owen had converted to Spiritualism late in life, following a sitting with an American medium called Mrs Hayden, who travelled to Britain in the 1840s to become the first working Spiritualist outside the United States and who was clearly a great hit. Indeed, she paved the way for Spiritualism in Europe.

Meanwhile, poor Emma Hardinge Britten found she did not have the stomach for the vilification she received at the hands of America's religious communities and eventually departed her adopted land for England, where the social atmosphere was already rather more tolerant.

Her Spiritualist career thrived and, as enthusiasm for this new phenomenon spread across the English-speaking world, she embarked on lengthy tours of both Australia and New Zealand.

Her final claim to fame is that she founded the first weekly Spiritualist magazine, entitled Two Worlds, in 1887. The National Spiritualists Federation, Britain's first official Spiritualist organisation, was established shortly afterwards, in 1890.

The Victorian Cult of Death

Britain was perhaps more open to Spiritualist ideas because of the Victorian Cult of Death. Queen Victoria, who reigned from 1837 till her death in 1901, was bereaved early in life and, many said at the time and still do today, grieved for her husband Prince Albert, who died in 1861, excessively. Retreating to her beloved Scottish idyll at Balmoral, she wore full mourning for the remaining forty years of her life and would have withdrawn from public life entirely if her Prime Minister had not warned her that such a move could imperil the standing of the monarchy in the eyes of the public.

Was she the inspiration for her era's obsession with mortality? To an extent, certainly. This imposing figure – this sombre queen draped in widow's weeds – chimed with an age where, despite the dawn of major medical advances, infant mortality remained devastatingly high and life expectancy low. Death stalked everyone, even the very rich, even the queen herself, and many attendant rituals were developed during her reign.

A widow was expected to mourn her spouse for a whole year, while a mother would mourn a lost baby for nine months, followed by three months of half-mourning. The household clocks were stopped during that period, and the mirrors draped in black crepe. Amongst the wealthier classes, tombstones and mausoleums became hugely important and many of the nation's most impressive cemeteries, including the Necropolis behind Glasgow's St Mungo's Cathedral, were constructed during the Victorian era.

Death, far from being a taboo subject, became something that everybody lived with. The dear departed were remembered at every turn and from this sprang the age's fascination with post-mortem life.

Spiritualism did seem to offer something more concrete, in the form of a direct communication with the dead. The traditional image of the Victorian parlour séance, with its wildly flickering candle-flames, sinuous shadows and weird, disembodied voices may set the hairs on the back of the neck on end, but their purpose was not to scare, rather it was to reassure and bring comfort.

Spiritualism also had a social advantage over the established faiths. It was more inclusive, particularly of women, and less learned. Women, according to the beliefs of the time, were actually considered to be more conducive to the spirit world, and more likely to have psychic sensibilities.

Unsurprisingly, Spiritualism became typically known as the pastime of wealthy housewives, and the séance became a realm in which women, for once, were dominant.

An interesting footnote is that Queen Victoria is alleged to have been assisted in communicating with her much-missed husband through the agency of her trusted and loyal Scottish ghillie, John Brown. Indeed, it is said that those of Celtic blood have a natural affinity with the world beyond.

daniel dunlas home (1833–1886)

Of the early Spiritualist pioneers, the name of Daniel Dunlas Home stands out. Born in Edinburgh in 1833, this troubled young man grew up to become an internationally renowned physical medium whose demonstrations of levitation are the stuff of legend.

Home's family, like many in those days, upped sticks and emigrated to America in 1842, in search of a better life and prospects. Things did not turn out well for them, with Home's mother dying in 1850, leaving him to the tender care of his sole remaining aunt. His mother was possessed of a certain psychic ability but Home was too young for her to have passed on her skills and knowledge by the time she died. However, it seems he inherited her sixth sense nonetheless.

As a teenager, strange, poltergeist-like activity began to occur in the house he shared with his aunt. Furniture moved of its own accord, objects flew from one side of the room to the next, and odd, inexplicable noises were heard day and night. Poltergeist activity is often associated with unhappy youngsters and Home definitely fitted into that category, but this phenomenon had another cause, as his aunt was about to discover.

She called in a priest, hoping he could exorcise the house of what she imagined to be some kind of demon. Instead he surprised her by deducing that the source of the problem was the boy's psychic abilities and that the solution was to control and develop his skills.

She must have taken his advice because, by the time he reached young adulthood, Home was an established medium on the Spiritualist circuit. He travelled throughout the United States, holding séances at which tables would shake, vibrate and even lift off the floor and spirits would send long, complex messages through a code of sharp raps. Even more astounding were the hands that would miraculously materialise in mid-air and set about penning messages on the sheets of notepaper that were always available, and the musical instruments that would suddenly appear and play themselves. In 1852, he pulled off the feat of actually levitating himself.

No wonder Home's appearances prompted eager queues round the block. And no wonder he aroused the suspicion of sceptics, eager to prove him a fraud.

In 1855, Home returned to Britain, where he gave fantastic demonstrations of levitation and psychic communication at sittings in London, including with the first of his calling, Kate Fox.

Home was a trance medium which meant that, upon commencing a sitting, he would fall into a somnambulistic state, from which he could only be roused very slowly. Whilst in one of these trances, on December 13, 1868, he performed his most famous demonstration of levitation. He was holding a sitting in London, in the top floor room of a patron's house. He entered his trance as usual and shortly afterwards, to the amazement of his onlookers, rose up bodily from his chair and sailed elegantly out of the open window. Outside, he hovered over the quiet, suburban street for some minutes before flying back through the window from whence he had come and returning to his seat.

It need hardly be said that this event caused a sensation amongst the chattering classes of London and made the opponents of Spiritualism even more determined to unmask him as the charlatan they believed he surely was.

Step forward Sir William Crookes, an esteemed doctor and president of the aforementioned Society for Psychical Research. He approached his subject with the objectivity of the scientist and conducted a series of rigorous tests to ascertain, once and for all, the integrity of Daniel Dunlas Home. He found no evidence whatever of fakery or illusion and could only conclude that Home was either a man way ahead of his time in terms of trickery, or he was for real.

However, to this day there remain those who regard Home as a conman of the first order, pointing to his early retirement at the age of 40 as indicative of the fact that only a young man could pull of such convincing stunts.

That said, even Harry Houdini, an arch-sceptic with, nevertheless, a long-standing fascination with Spiritualism, could never replicate Home's incredible levitations and moving furniture spectacles.

This flying Scotsman died in 1886, of tuberculosis.

aRtHuR cONaN ðoyLe

Arthur Conan Doyle was born in Edinburgh in 1859 and is perhaps best known as the creator of the fictional detective Sherlock Holmes. But Sir Arthur, as he became after serving in the Boer War of 1899–1902, is also famous for being one of the great champions of Spiritualism. To many he is regarded as something akin to the St Paul of the Spiritualist movement.

Such was his faith in the endurance of the human spirit after death, and his enthusiasm for a religion that incorporated actual communication with these departed spirits, that he forfeited much of his credibility in the eyes of his peers and contemporaries. To Conan Doyle this did not matter, Spiritualism was a faith that endured to the very end and brought him great peace and comfort.

He had a difficult start in life. Though born of moderately wealthy parents, his civil servant father suffered from epilepsy and increasingly acute alcoholism. His mother Mary, however, was his guiding light. A great storyteller, he recalled her voice "sinking to a horror-stricken whisper" as she neared the conclusion of one of her captivating stories. To the young Arthur, stories were a vital diversion from the otherwise chaotic character of his early home life.

He was sent to a Jesuit school as a youngster and quickly came to hate its brutal regime. He later lost his religious conviction, declaring himself an agnostic. Such was his integrity that, as a young adult struggling to get a start in the medical profession, he refused to enlist the help of his father's friends because these were Roman Catholic church connections and he felt it would be wrong to exploit them. This robustness of character was one of Conan Doyle's outstanding features.

Upon leaving Stonyhurst College which, if nothing else, furnished him with a fruitful panoply of characters which were later incorporated into his works of fiction, Conan Doyle entered the School of Medicine at Edinburgh University.

His early career as a doctor took place aboard various ships and in the towns of Plymouth and Portsmouth. However, he was also pursuing a parallel career as a writer and in 1887 and to enormous acclaim, published his first Sherlock Holmes story, A Study In Scarlet. In 1891, he was sufficiently successful to take the plunge into a full-time writing career and by the 1920s, he was one of the most celebrated and highly paid novelists of his period.

But this hard-earned literary life was to be rudely interrupted, causing Conan Doyle to change direction once again. First came the Boer War. He was 40 and therefore too old to enlist but this did not deter Conan Doyle from assisting in a cause in which he believed deeply. He volunteered to work in a field hospital, where he witnessed appalling suffering and death. In his memoir, The Great Boer War, he described seeing more people die of typhoid as a result of the hopelessly inadequate hygiene than of war wounds. The sight of so much waste, so much death, affected him deeply.

In 1906, his first wife Louisa died. Then, the greatest blow of all: his son Kingsley, whose birth in 1892 he had described as "the chief event" of he and Louisa's life, died of pneumonia during the First World War.

Conan Doyle also lost his brother, two brothers-in-law and two nephews to this dreadful conflict.

It was these terrible experiences that undoubtedly sowed the seeds of Conan Doyle's subsequent devotion to Spiritualism.

The First World War

Interest in Spiritualism had peaked in the mid-19th century, when it counted as many as 11 million devotees worldwide. But by the dawn of the 20th century, its popularity was already fading as the upper and middle classes found other amusements and the half-lit world of the séance began to seem hopelessly Victorian and old-fashioned.

The fact that the Spiritualist movement was disastrously disorganised and factionalised, and that the Spiritualist circuit was awash with fraudsters charging extortionate fees and offering feats that would not have been out of place in a Music Hall performance further accounts for the movement's rapid decline.

But the First World War changed all that, and prompted a huge revival of Spiritualism, particularly amongst the working classes.

The War to End All Wars, as it was briefly known, broke out in 1914 and quickly became a world-scale conflict and arguably the most brutal mankind had ever seen. Never had so many soldiers been called up, from all across the class spectrum, nor so many slaughtered in action, many would say needlessly and as a result of poor direction on the part of the officers. "Lions led by donkeys" is how the spectacle of brave young foot soldiers being sent to their deaths by ignorant upper-class officers was later to be described.

Over nine million were killed on the battlefield in the course of this four-year war, and as many again died as a result of genocide, starvation and bombing raids.

Hundreds upon thousands of women were left widowed, with young children to raise alone, as whole generations were wiped out at a stroke. Small villages were left with no young men at all, farms struggled on without sons, industry without male apprentices. People lost count of the dead; it was on an unimaginable scale.

Thus it seems natural that these suddenly bereft, desperately grieving people would seek means of saying goodbye to the loved ones so rudely snatched away from them, and Spiritualism offered a route. The séance and sitting flourished during and after the War years, as mediumship again went into ascendancy.

One of the primary attractions that Spiritualism held for Conan

Doyle was that, if it was true, then it meant his beloved son existed somewhere still.

From sceptic to believer

Conan Doyle's interest in Spiritualism dated as far back as 1881, when he was prevailed upon to attend a lecture on the subject. He went on to describe this event in an article for *The Light*, a leading Spiritualist periodical. However, at that time, his feet were firmly planted in the sceptics camp.

Later, when he was working in Southsea, he attended a series of séances at the home of a General Drayson, a teacher at the nearby Greenwich Naval College and one of Conan Doyle's patients. The Medium in attendance was a railway signalman with, it appears, remarkable powers of physical mediumship. Tables trembled, objects flew, weird creatures materialised in mid-air. It was, frankly, all too much for the young, pragmatic Edinburgh doctor, who left with the distinct impression that someone was having a joke at his expense.

Nevertheless, the experience kindled his interest in the supernatural.

In the February of 1889, Conan Doyle, who was nothing if not possessed of a thirsty mind, attended a lecture on mesmerism, given by a Professor Milo de Meyer, who attempted to mesmerise, amongst others, Conan Doyle, unsuccessfully as it happened.

These were exciting times for students of the human mind. Sigmund Freud had discovered the subconscious, the arts of hypnosis and mesmerism were being utilised in the pursuit of further discoveries and mental illness was being re-evaluated in the light of modern medical knowledge.

In 1894, having joined the esteemed Society for Psychical Research some years before, Conan Doyle, alongside Dr Sydney Scott and Frank Podmore, took part in his first psychic investigation.

A Colonel Elmore, living in Dorset, had reported a disturbing case to the Society. His wife and daughter, he said, had been hearing mysterious noises during the night, including a rather chilling moaning call and the sound of chains being dragged along the floor by person or persons unknown. Not only that but the family dog now refused to enter certain rooms and most of the domestic staff had taken fright and left.

Suitably intrigued, the three man team despatched to Dorset, where they spent a night attempting to record the "fearsome noise" that ensued and to trace its source. It was certainly a hair-raising experience but their experiments were inconclusive. Conan Doyle, however, was convinced that something untoward and possibly supernatural had occurred.

This gut feeling was compounded when, many years later, the long deceased body of a ten year old was unearthed in the garden. The record does not show whether the Elmore hauntings ceased upon this discovery, but Conan Doyle was certain that it was the source of the disturbances.

Conan Doyle was also involved in further investigations, a series of which convinced him that telepathy existed between sympathetic souls. Ever studious, he continued to study the phenomenon of Spiritualism, finally hitting upon a book called *Human Personality and its Survival of Bodily Death*, written by the Cambridge Classics scholar and founder member of the Society for Psychical Research, Frederick WH Meyer. This profound work greatly influenced Conan Doyle's thinking and is still a literary touchstone of the Spiritualist movement.

Several mediums are said to have received messages from the irrepressible Meyer from beyond the grave, often relating to intellectual matters such as those outlined in his signature work.

The death of his son accelerated Conan Doyle's examination and, a year later, he was rewarded when a Welsh medium brought forth a message from the young man. It was a profoundly moving and welcome experience and Conan Doyle believed firmly that it had been Kingsley's voice he heard, speaking of "concerns unknown to the medium". Another time, he encountered his long lost mother Mary, and one of his nephews, who materialised before his eyes "as plainly as I ever saw them in my life!" thanks to the efforts of a physical medium.

Sceptics, however, maintained that these were the distortions of a grief-stricken mind. In short, that Conan Doyle saw what he craved to see and nothing more.

In 1917, after much careful consideration, Conan Doyle went

public about his belief in Spiritualism, addressing a lecture to the London Spiritual Alliance in October of that year. This speech went on to form the basis of his book The New Revelation, published a year later, when he and his second wife embarked upon a world tour of lectures, encompassing Canada, Australia and New Zealand.

This public statement of belief was the scandal of its day, and caused many to think the poor man had gone mad. But even the most cynical concluded that, whatever the truth of the matter, Conan Doyle was sincere in his beliefs. Harry Price, one of the great investigators into psychic phenomena, who made it his business to unmask fakers and fraudsters – and a very profitable business it was too – said of Conan Doyle: "His extreme credulity ... was the despair of his colleagues."

Doyle and the Cottingley Fairies

This queasiness in the face of Conan Doyle's convictions was exacerbated by the case of the Cottingley Fairies. In 1920, Conan Doyle was fascinated to hear of a series of photographic images taken by two young women, living in Cottingley, Yorkshire, apparently of fairies at the bottom of their garden. Elsie Wright, 16, and her school friend Frances Griffiths, 10, had taken a number of photographs of what appeared to be perfect little fairies, complete with diaphonous wings and tiny, doll-life features. Indeed, they so resembled the Victorian picture-book version of ladylike fairies, as opposed to the traditional Celtic image of rough, hairy folk with dark powers, that Conan Doyle should have known better.

Alas, he did not, and went so far as to publish an article in *The Strand* magazine describing the images as unquestionably authentic. Kodak film laboratories were not so sure. Though they confirmed that the images were neither double exposures nor had the negatives been tampered with, they were also able to confirm that the "special effects" could be reproduced with ease.

It seems that these two English girls had pulled a stunt that rapidly got out of hand. Sixty years later, they confessed, though their handiwork had long since been exposed as fakery. Something of which most onlookers had not really needed convincing.

Houdini

That same year, Conan Doyle met the master illusionist Harry Houdini who, as previously mentioned, had a huge, if arms-length, interest in Spiritualism. Following the death of his mother, Mme Weiss, to whom some say he was unnaturally close, Houdini was pitched into a welter of grief, from which he never truly recovered. In the immediate wake of her passing, he sought out medium after medium, hoping to make contact with her. Instead he discovered, to his great horror, that most of the mediums he encountered were crude tricksters, more practised in the art of exploiting people's grief than communing with the dear departed. That set him off on another mission – to debunk Spiritualism once and for all.

Surprisingly then, Houdini and Conan Doyle became great friends. Houdini was greatly appreciative of Doyle's open, honest and earnest personality, describing him as at least "one intelligent person" associated with this damnable art. He asked Conan Doyle to prove that Spiritualism was for real and the great writer naturally accepted the challenge.

Thus, in 1922, they met up in Atlantic City along with their wives. Conan Doyle's second wife, Jean was a psychic herself, transmitting messages from the other side through automatic or "inspired" writing. She served as the medium at the ensuing séance, during which she contacted Houdini's mother, passing on her messages to her son in written English.

Houdini was unimpressed. For a start, Mme Weiss could not speak English, conversing in her native Hungarian right up until her dying day. Furthermore, she failed to mention to the Medium that this particular day was her birthday; something that would never have slipped her mind during her lifetime!

Lady Jean attempted to dismiss these concerns, arguing that the messages of spirits are always transmitted in a language that the medium understands and that Mme Weiss would have little truck with birthdays now she was on the other side. This only incensed Houdini, who left the meeting deeply troubled.

The Conan Doyle–Houdini friendship was subsequently strained to breaking point when the former attacked the latter in the press, accusing him of actually being a medium himself, hence his zeal to debunk Spiritualism. Doyle explained that Houdini did not perform amazing feats of human endeavour but simply achieved his escapes through "dematerialising" in one place and rematerialising in another.

Houdini responded angrily, saying Conan Doyle was "senile" and continued in his crusade against what he considered dark arts indeed, culminating in the publication, in 1924, of A Magician Amongst the Spiritualists, in which he exposed many of the prominent mediums of his day.

For his part, Conan Doyle was unshaken in his beliefs. He died in 1930 of heart disease, writing on the eve of his passing: "The reader will judge that I have had many adventures. The greatest and most glorious of all awaits me now."

Helen Duncan, "Hellish Nell"

If Arthur Conan Doyle was the St Paul of the Spiritualist movement, then Helen Duncan was the St Joan, in that she suffered deeply for her art and died a premature and pitiful death.

Born in the small, picturesque village of Callander, near Loch Lomond, in Scotland, Helen Duncan was to become one of the most famous physical mediums in history and was the last woman ever to be tried, and convicted, under the Witchcraft Act of 1735.

Her life began simply enough. She was born on November 25, 1897, the daughter of a slate-maker and builder and the fourth of eight children. During her rather frugal childhood, she had a number of clairvoyant experiences, which her mother warned her not to speak about in public. Helen, whose tomboy behaviour had earned her the nickname Hellish Nell, brought further disgrace to her family when, at the age of 16, she fell pregnant without a husband in sight. She was thus banished from her small town home to Dundee, where she worked in one of the city's many jute mills and lived in a women's hostel. After a period in a sanitorium, where she was treated for tuberculosis, she worked as an auxiliary at Dundee Royal Infirmary, working predominantly in the psychiatric wing.

It was in Dundee that she met her future husband Henry, who had been invalided out of the army with rheumatic fever, an ailment that set the precedent for his future, chronic ill health. Like Helen, Henry was a "sensitive" with a profound and intellectual interest in Spiritualism. Because of his ill health, he was often unable to work. Instead, he devoted much of his time to reading Spiritualist literature and using his accumulated knowledge to assist his wife in developing her skill.

Though there was little time for that. Times were very tough for this young couple, Helen endured no less than twelve pregnancies, of which only six children survived. She worked for a time in a local bleach factory, an awful, health-impairing way to make a living, while working as a medium in the evenings.

From the start then, we can see that mediumship was a way of earning money for Duncan; a fact that caused many to be suspicious of her, not least because, the more spectacular her sittings, the more she coined it in.

However it should be noted that, if raising the dead was lucrative, then so too was debunking the art of Spiritualism. Not all of Duncan's critics had the intregrity of Harry Houdini; some were just out for a good story to sell to the popular press for a fat fee. Unsurprisingly, the hard-working Helen was often incensed by her detractors, and would physically lash out at loud-mouthed sceptics who attended her sittings.

What should be remembered is that, like most of her clientele, Helen Duncan was a bitterly poor woman who struggled to survive, aided only to a small extent by her husband, due to his general unfitness for work. Dumpy, poorly-dressed and matter-of-fact, she was like thousands of working class women, many of whom were left widowed by the war and thrown on their own resources, and this was at a time when women were paid substantially less than men for the same labour.

Her mediumship offered solace in these bleak lives, a glimpse not only of peace to come in the hereafter but a chance to speak to those who had passed over and to bask for a while in the past. Thus what has been described as her somewhat mercenary approach to Spiritualism – she expected to be paid, and decently – was not frowned upon by the majority of her patrons. A woman had to make a living, after all.

Can the camera lie?

Her mediumship was also, without doubt, a performance in itself.

Once immersed in a trance state, ectoplasm would begin to emanate from her body, sometimes from her nostrils, sometimes her mouth. On one occasion, according to a witness, it actually seemed to "spurt from the nipples of her breasts". This curious material, never satisfactorily analysed, would coagulate in mid-air, finally resolving into the figure of a spirit from the other side.

One photograph, alleged to have been taken at a Helen Duncan séance, shows the spirit form of an elderly man, rendered visible by ectoplasm, which gives the appearance of his being draped in a thick white sheet. Though his body is pretty much entirely concealed, the details of his face are remarkably rendered.

This eerie figure seems to emanate from the side of the medium's head, to which it is connected by a kind of ectoplasmic umbilical cord.

Speaking many years later at Helen Duncan's trial, Hannen Swaffer, a renowned Fleet Street journalist of his day and the founder of the Spiritualist weekly *Psychic News*, declared that anyone who mistook ectoplasm for butter muslin, a common charge, "would be a child. Under a red light in a séance room it would look yellow or pink whilst these spirit forms all displayed a white appearance."

The photographic evidence, such as it is, seems to bear Swaffer's assertion out, revealing spirits of a ghastly white pallor.

Duncan was assisted in her remarkable work by her spirit guide, a rather snooty, elegant gentleman called Albert who nonetheless channelled a considerable array of other-wordly guests her way.

In demand

Word soon spread regarding this remarkable woman, and it was not long before people across the country were clamouring to see her. During the 1930s and 40s, she began touring the country, hosting public meetings at Spiritualist churches, village halls and private houses. As the Second World War began to ratchet up horrendous numbers of casualties, so the demand for a contact with the recently departed increased. At this time, estimates suggest there were upward of a million active Spiritualists in Britain alone, over a thousand Spiritualist churches and several thousand home circles, the latter being the smaller-scale, more domestic setting for a séance.

Wherever she went, Helen Duncan did not disappoint – the dead rose up before the living as if by magic, imparting messages so detailed and accurate that onlookers could only gasp. How, they wondered, could this ordinary looking, middle-aged Scottish housewife be capable of such amazing feats?

A widower called Vincent Woodcock attended one of Duncan's sittings, along with his sister-in-law, and was converted to Spiritualism by what he witnessed. Helen Duncan did not merely pass on a message from Woodcock's dead wife, she caused her to materialise in their midst in a wave of ectoplasm. This phantom then took off her wedding ring and placed it on her sister's finger, saying: "It is my wish that this takes place for the sake of my little girl."

All of which was music to the ears of Woodcock and his sister-in-law, who subsequently married, returning years later to another Helen Duncan séance. The dead wife obligingly reappeared, this time to bestow her blessings on the new union.

Woodcock was one of the many grateful clients who testified in Duncan's favour at her trial, held at the Old Bailey in London in 1944. But more of that later.

Major JH Webster MBE, in his book *Voices of the Past*, recounts two incredible materialisations at the hands of Helen Duncan.

In 1942, during the summer, the Scottish Medium held a séance in Manchester at which a Mr Ramsden, a Squadron Leader in the RAF, was in attendance. Though a keen student of Spiritualism, he was yet to be fully persuaded as to its authenticity.

The séance began as normal, with prayers and a hymn or two. The curtains were then drawn and Duncan descended into a trance. Within minutes, ectoplasm began to emerge from her body, forming an eerily opaque, moon-coloured cloud in mid-air. Gradually, the refined features of Albert, her spirit guide, began to distinguish themselves.

He addressed himself, without ceremony or hesitation, to the startled Mr Ramsden, who had booked himself in under a false name. Albert, it seems, was not fooled for a minute and announced that there was a woman waiting in the spiritual wings who was desperately impatient to meet with him again.

This woman transpired to be Mr Ramsden's mother, who soon afterwards appeared, as if in the flesh. Rather tongue-tied at first, she confessed that, "I have been waiting for this moment for years, and now I am here I feel too excited to know what to say."

Nevertheless, she did relate enough private family information to convince her son that what he was witnessing was more than a mere figment of his imagination.

Perhaps more startling still is the epilogue to this little story. In conversation with him afterwards, Helen Duncan revealed to Mr Ramsden that she never saw the spirit forms herself, indeed had never seen a spirit form in her life. "I am sure that if I did then I would die of fright," she told him.

At a subsequent séance, in March 1943, Duncan accurately transmitted messages to what was a very international audience in a variety of languages of which she had no previous knowledge. Duncan had barely attended school, and gone to work very hard and very early; how could she therefore have a working knowledge, all of a sudden, of Afrikaans, a Bolivian Spanish dialect, Polish and Dutch?

At this same sitting, Duncan also brought forth the spirit form of a recently killed New Zealander pilot. His Wing Commander, a guest of Mr Ramsden, could only gasp his astonishment.

Bill Watson, the deceased airman, went on to describe the nature of his death, pinpointing the cause to his inability to use his escape hatch. His Commander, suddenly regaining control of himself, demanded to know more and Watson was only too happy to oblige. His technical knowledge, the listeners insisted, far surpassed anything that Helen Duncan could have picked up.

In fact, it is claimed that this Wing Commander later instigated a programme of modifications to the model of aircraft used by the tragic airman. And along the lines suggested by Mr Watson's ghostly debriefing.

A challenge

Mediumship was an insecure profession. Even someone of Helen Duncan's fame was subject to fashionable changes of heart, and thus she took up every paying opportunity that presented itself. Like Arthur Conan Doyle before her, she presented herself at the London Spiritualist Alliance, though she shied away from intellectualising her work, preferring the direct approach of actual mediumship.

She also, and perhaps unwisely, took up the challenge laid down by Harry Price, the arch-sceptic, and former member of the Society for Psychical Research. He left this organisation to form his own, the National Laboratory of Psychical Research.

Malcolm Gaskill, in his book *Hellish Nell: Last of Britain's Witches*, describes the intrusive manner in which Price set about Helen Duncan. First, two doctors were enlisted to conduct a physical examination, to determine whether she secreted objects or materials about her person. To all intents and purposes, it was as humiliating and invasive as the kind of strip-search conducted in prisons to ensure inmates are not carrying illegal drugs.

Next, she was rudely awoken from a trance by someone shouting in her face. Meanwhile the ecotoplasm that was beginning to emanate from her person was snatched for analysis.

This analysis revealed Duncan's ectoplasm to be composed primarily of egg-white and woodpulp while a series of X-rays revealed her incredible ability to swallow and regurgitate, at will, the materials required for her performances. Harry Price thus concluded that Duncan was "one of the cleverest frauds in the history of Spiritualism".

The records of the Helen Duncan séances conducted at the National Laboratory of Psychic Research, with observations by a number of leading academics, were published by Harry Price in 1931 in a single volume, entitled *Regurgitation and the Duncan Mediumship*.

Duncan was deeply shaken both by Price's rough conduct and his damning conclusions. Yet the Spiritualist movement was unshaken in its faith in her and the work continued.

A hugely popular magician of the day, Will Goldston, insisted that the effects produced at a Helen Duncan séance were not replicable, even by a man of his considerable skills. Such tributes gave Duncan heart.

Alec Harris, a notable Welsh medium, was convinced of the truth of Spiritualism, despite a very orthodox, Christian upbringing in the Rhondda Valley, by a visit to one of Duncan's séances. His sister Connie had recently died and he was both gratified and deeply shaken when she appeared to him as if from nowhere.

Connie not only greeted and reassured him, she also urged her brother to recognise his psychic abilities and to develop and use them. Which he most certainly did, going on to become one of the most successful mediums of his day.

Everything changes

But the event that was to turn Duncan's life upside down took place in Portsmouth, in 1941, though it was at a later séance in 1944 that the full force of the law began to bear down upon her.

The town was home to Britain's naval fleet and, as such, a target for the German Luftwaffe. Thus we can be assured that the war was very much on the minds of everyone who attended Helen Duncan's séance on the night of the 19th January 1944. Well, perhaps not everyone. In the midst of the credulous audience sat a police officer in plain clothes, there on a twelve-and-a-half shilling ticket, purchased for him by a naval officer called Lieutenant R Worth, who believed Duncan to be of the lowest order of common trickster.

What caused his ire? Possibly that, in 1941, Duncan had called forth the spirit of a young sailor who explained to his attendant mother that he had been killed when his ship, HMS Barham, went down on November 25, 1941. This was a profound shock to the mother and, as news of this ghastly revelation got out, came as something of a rude surprise to the Admiralty too, who were yet to release details of the sinking of the warship. Could Duncan, some wondered, be a spy? Suffice it to say that Duncan's activities were of enough concern to attract the attention of MI5, who were instrumental in building the case against her.

Doubtless a strong dose of wartime hysteria infected proceedings because, in all likelihood, Duncan's mediumship was not half as accurate as people were later lead to believe. It is not beyond the realms of possibility that an anxious mother named the ship and that, when Duncan produced the son's name, they both put two and two together and made four. A warship sinking in wartime is hardly an unwarranted guess. And almost certainly, the story grew arms and legs in the telling.

In one version, by way of an example, the dead sailor appears wearing a cap on which is clearly brandished the legend, HMS Barham. Not only that, but we hear that Helen Duncan's subsequent arrest was on the express orders of none other than Winston Churchill, the very man who later branded the whole business of the trial absurd.

Whatever happened exactly, the events of January 1941 ensured that Duncan's activities were closely monitored thereafter, concluding with this fateful night in 1944.

As was often the case, in the course of the sitting, ectoplasm began to emanate from Duncan. In appearance, it looked like a large, floating white sheet. The police officer, assuming that that is exactly what it was, jumped up from his chair and grabbed at it, causing it to vanish into thin air. Or rather, as her supporters maintained, to snap back into her body, an action that happened much too fast and caused her body to be scarred with nasty friction burns. A fingertip search of the room, conducted immediately afterwards, uncovered neither a white sheet nor any other incriminating or even suspicious paraphernalia. Indeed, it was customary for Duncan, prior to every sitting, to allow herself to be thoroughly strip-searched, in an ante-room attended by women only, in order to throw off the oft-heard accusation that she concealed objects and material about her person to assist in her performances.

But back to the fateful night of 1944; after failing to grab hold of the ectoplasm, the officer then roused Helen Duncan abruptly from her trance, a move that her friends claimed did her irreparable damage as mediums should always be allowed to emerge from their trances in their own time. Finally, she was arrested, as were three of her sitters, presumed by the officer to be "plants" seeded into the audience to enhance the fraud.

Portsmouth Magistrates Court subsequently charged all four under the Vagrancy Act. Had they been convicted of this charge, they would each have incurred a five-shilling fine. Despite the relatively minor nature of the charge against her, Duncan was refused bail and sent down to Holloway, the notoriously unpleasant women's prison in London. Whilst there on remand, Duncan learnt that the charge against her had been upgraded to one of Conspiracy which, during times of war, carried with it the death penalty. This charge was later amended to one of Witchcraft as per the 1735 act. Under this ancient law, considered by most practising legal people to be all but obsolete, she was charged on the grounds that it was unlawful to "exercise or use human conjuration that through the agency of Helen Duncan, spirits of deceased dead persons should appear to be present".

She was also accused of Larceny, "by falsely pretending she was in a position to bring about the appearances of then spirits of deceased persons".

The Spiritualist community, both in Scotland and throughout the world, were up in arms about these charges and a defence fund was quickly established in order to underwrite the travelling expenses of witnesses to her sterling character from all corners of the globe.

The Law Societies of both Scotland and England declared the trial a travesty of justice. They were not alone in their outrage. On hearing of the case, wartime Prime Minister Winston Churchill, who had an interest in Spiritualism himself, wrote to Herbert Morrison at the Home Office demanding: "Let me have a report on why the Witchcraft Act, 1735, was used in a modern Court of Justice. What was the cost of this trial to the State, observing that witnesses were brought from Portsmouth and maintained here in this crowded London, for a fortnight, and the Recorder kept busy with all this obsolete tomfoolery, to the detriment of necessary work in the Courts?"

All this notwithstanding, the trial went ahead, lasting seven days in all and feeding the insatiable tabloid press with lurid story after lurid story.

Amongst those who flocked to testify on Duncan's behalf was Kathleen McNeill, a Glasgow housewife, who told the court how her sister had materialised at a séance. Given that she had died only hours previously it was inconceivable, said McNeill, that Helen Duncan had any foreknowledge. Only her spirit guide Albert could have imparted such information.

Alfred Dodd, an academic and the author of a number of learned works on Shakespeare's sonnets, described how he was brought face to face with his deceased grandfather through the agency of Ms Duncan. This ancient, portly gentleman appeared, as he had in life, wearing a smoking cap from which his familiar donkey fringe protruded. After conversing with his grandson some moments, he turned to Alfred's friend Tom, who was sitting beside him, and said: "Look into my face and into my eyes. Ask Alfred to show you my portrait. It is the same man."

James Herries, a journalist on the respected broadsheet *The Scotsman*, and a Justice of the Peace into the bargain, related how Duncan called forth the spirit of the late lamented Arthur Conan Doyle.

They may as well have saved their breath because Helen Duncan was convicted under the ludicrous charges and sent down.

Duncan's defence team had urged her to demonstrate her powers before the court but the Court refused to allow this. The latter wanted her to testify, a request she refused on the grounds that the alleged incidents took place while she was in a state of deep trance. This meant that she would, could, have no recollection of them.

The judge, after a weekend of deliberation, declared that the Court's business was not to ascertain whether "genuine manifestations of this kind are possible" but rather, to determine whether the accused had acted dishonestly. The Court, he said, had concluded that she had, and he handed down a ten-month sentence.

Helen Duncan is said to have wept bitter tears on hearing this, declaring: "I never hee'd so mony lies in a' my life."

She served rather less than the prescribed ten months, but emerged from prison shaken by the experience and with her health, never good in the first place, severely impaired.

During her time in prison, Duncan's supporters attempted an appeal, but it was thrown out by the House of Lords. It was clear that the British establishment was thoroughly embarrassed by the whole sorry force.

Duncan's supporters also clamoured for a change in the law and got that at least. In 1951, the 1735 Witchcraft Act was finally removed from the statute books and replaced by the Fraudulent Mediums Act. This law, in contrast to its quasi-medieval predecessor, was contemptuous rather than fearful of the supernatural. It equated mediumship with showbusiness and concerned itself solely with whether or not money changed hands. If it was done for free, it was deemed harmless entertainment.

Meanwhile, on the inside, Duncan continued to work as a

medium, with the warders and prisoners comprising her new clientele. One apocryphal story is that Winston Churchill himself visited her in Holloway, apparently to seek out her services. This, however, receives no confirmation from official sources. In fact, his outrage with regards to the trial appears to be his only contact point with the life and times of Helen Duncan.

Upon her release, and despite previously insisting that she would not, Duncan resumed her Spiritualist career, though on a much lesser scale than before. The lurid publicity of the trial, coupled with the stain of incarceration, had tarnished her image in the eyes of the public. Not only that, but her psychic abilities appeared to be evaporating to the extent that the official Spiritualist body, the National Union of Spiritualists, eventually revoked her license.

Though she continued to scrape a halfway decent living, Duncan was still subject to police raids, including one in Nottingham in 1956. Such was the shock she received on this occasion that she died five weeks later, aged only 59, after an exhausting lifetime of hard graft and endless, often vicious criticism.

But the story does not quite end there. Helen Duncan remains a revered figure within the Spiritualist community, and is regarded by many as a martyr to the cause. She had made a number of notable appearances at modern séances, including one in which materialised before her daughter Gina, through the agency of the medium Rita Goold.

Should we really be surprised to hear that this extraordinary Scottish housewife, breadwinner and mother should still be making appearances at séances, albeit from the other side?

aLbert best

Albert Best was born in Belfast, on 2nd December 1917, though he spent the majority of his later life in Glasgow. An intensely private individual, he was widowed young and subsequently lived alone. However, through his mediumship, he reached out to thousands of people, and his contribution to the world of Spiritualism is considerable.

Best was brought up by a woman who was not his grandmother

but did go by the name of Mrs Best, his mother having died when he was still a boy. It was a rather austere and not particularly happy childhood, by all accounts though, Albert did have one thing in common with his elderly guardian: a psychic gift.

As with most mediums, Albert's first encounter with the other side occurred when he was very young and it left him baffled. Aged seven, he met a man brandishing a lamp on the stairs. Curiously, he had string tied round each knee. Naturally alarmed, Albert rushed to point the figure out to Mrs Best, who responded by telling him he was seeing things. However, as soon as she thought he was out of earshot, she addressed the mysterious figure as "Father", urging him to go away as he was "frightening the boy".

A natural talent

It was a few years before Albert began to get to grips with his unusual talent. Rosalind Cattanach, a friend of Best's and one of the few people to have gathered much in the way of biographical detail regarding the famous Medium, recounts how, during his teens, he got talking to a window cleaner who invited him to attend his local Spiritualist church. Which Best did, only to be told by the attendant medium that, one day, he would don an army uniform and travel to Africa. For a working-class lad from Belfast, this was the equivalent of being told he would don a spacesuit and travel to the moon; he left distinctly underwhelmed, though he never forgot her words.

During this period, Albert was experiencing a deeply disturbing phenomenon. He kept hearing a voice, which seemed to emanate from within his own head. This voice gave him advice and made suggestions as to what he should do next. He was troubled by it, as you can imagine. Perhaps he feared he was going mad, or developing some sort of split personality. Yet the voice itself, far from sounding evil or demented, was very reassuring. Still, he was terrified that other people could hear it and he would take himself off into the country on his days off – by then he was employed at a ropeworks, having left school at 14 – so that he could commune with the voice without having to worry about being overheard.

A few years later, the mystery of the voice was solved for him. It seems to be the case with Spiritualism that it takes one to know one, and it was not until Best attended a Spiritualist church in Chichester that he encountered a medium who told him she could see lights all around him; a clear indication of strong psychic powers.

He went on to join a development circle, alongside his old friend the window cleaner.

Development circles

Development circles have been described as the "backbone of the Spiritualist movement" and anyone who is serious about developing their psychic skills is advised to attend a circle or seek out a sympathetic medium who can guide them.

The Spiritualist National Union is a good first port of call and most would-be psychics are encouraged to attend Spiritualist services for at least six months before even thinking about attending a development circle.

There are, of course, more secular versions, often called home circles, but novices should check out the credentials of the presiding medium first as, sadly, psychic charlatans did not die out with the Second World War.

Development circles are less religious in character than Spiritualist services. The group usually sits in a circle so that, physically, everyone is on an equal basis, and the session begins with a hymn or a meditation or even just an informal chat. The idea is that everyone feels relaxed and at home before the business of contacting the dead gets underway. Anyone who wishes to is encouraged to speak up if he or she detects a spirit presence or has a message to impart, but there is no pressure as every individual's psychic ability develops at a different pace.

These kinds of gatherings, overseen by a skilled and experienced psychic, are an essential first step for a medium as it allows the novice to ask questions about the various forms of mediumship and the terminology used, and to ask for tips on technique and talk though any personal experiences.

Many mediums hail from families where psychic abilities are commonplace and oft-discussed. These people can come to a development circle with a certain amount of confidence and foreknowledge. Others, like Albert Best, come to Spiritualism with very little experience of mediumship and may well be a little wary, even a little scared, of the whole subject. A strong, supportive development circle is therefore invaluable and it is not unusual to move from one to another, as Best apparently did, looking for the "right fit".

Developing a psychic gift requires a deal of patience. Even unusually gifted people like Best can take years to polish up their craft to the extent that they can serve their church and host public meetings. Some develop only so far, using their gift solely for private purposes.

This long apprenticeship is necessary to ensure that the new medium has confidence and consistency of approach and is able to distinguish between and accurately read even the most difficult of spirits.

Initially, mediums must learn how to clear their minds and use their senses to their utmost. Expecting phantoms and Native American spirit guides on the first night is not only unrealistic, it can lead to false imaginings and interfere with the real process of development.

One Glasgow Spiritualist to whom I spoke describes it as trying to achieve something akin to the Buddhist concept of contemplation.

"The human mind is a noisy place," he says, "only once it is free of all thoughts and expectations, can the spirit world make contact and expect to be heard."

The presence of an experienced medium is very important at the development stage because novices cannot always be sure that the spirits they draw are necessarily benign ones. A good guide can ensure that anything untoward is dealt with decisively.

Being a successful medium requires study, self-awareness and commitment. Not unlike any religion, when you come to think of it.

The second world war

When the second world war broke out, Best, then aged 22, signed up to the Inniskillen Fusiliers. The seemingly crazy prophecy made by the medium at his first Spiritualist meeting came true in 1940, when he was dispatched, wearing British Army uniform, to Algiers, in North Africa. It was a horrendous and dangerous campaign and whilst out there, a disturbing memory surfaced in Best's mind.

His real grandmother, whom he met only once, when he was in his teens, had said to him: "You'll be a widower before you are twenty-four. I haven't seen you all my life, but I'll be with you in Goubellet."

Goubellet Plain is in the north of Algiers, near the border of Tunis. Best's batallion was charged with the duty of clearing it in preparation for an Allied advance. It was a lethal job and Best, along with a number of his comrades, was left for dead, having been picked off by German soldiers looking down at them from a high ridge of land. Lying wounded, and perhaps ready to throw in the towel, Best heard a voice urging him to stand up and walk. Eventually he heeded it and was captured and taken to a prisoner-of-war camp.

Perhaps it was the same voice that had talked him through his lonely adolescence? Certainly it was one he trusted, even though it led him into the nightmarish experience of a wartime prison camp. That said, perhaps his guiding spirit knew he would survive this ordeal and go on to perform important work.

Best eventually returned home on a hospital ship, only to receive the most dreadful news of his life. During the blitz on Belfast, his young wife Rose and their three infant children had been killed outright. He did recover physically from his injuries, going on to serve his country again in Italy where he received further wounds, but he never recovered emotionally from the loss of his family.

This deep grief, which he carried with him all his life, was reflected in the enormous compassion he offered everyone who approached him for help. He knew only too well the bitter taste of sudden loss and the frustration of never having had the chance to say goodbye. Best was not alone in this of course. All across the world, in America, France, Germany, Britain, were people agonising over the deaths of their loved ones in war, and Spiritualism was enjoying a sudden surge in popularity, as the story of Helen Duncan testifies.

A friendly medium

However, it was a few years before Best took up work as a medium. In the interim, he left Belfast and settled in Scotland, where he took up a job as a postman; a calling that would stand him in good stead in the future. Best was not one of those mediums who uttered vague names and descriptions whilst glancing wildly round the room hoping someone would help him out. By contrast, he did not just get the names of his spirit visitors absolutely right, he was often able to fill in details as to exactly where they lived, right down to the house number. Once a postman ...

Best was a member of a number of development circles during the late 1940s and early 50s. It was during this period that the spirit world seemed to offer him the possibility of becoming a physical medium, though the story he told his friend Laurence Goss is anything but inspiring.

Best was sitting in a chair having a rest when, suddenly opening his eyes, he saw that ectoplasm was seeping from his eyes, mouth and nostrils and forming a cloud in the mid-air. Addressing the spirit world, he said firmly, "No, no, I don't want this" and the weird substance vanished. That, it seems, was the beginning and end of his career as a physical medium.

Instead, like most modern mediums, Best heard the voices of his spirit visitors and passed them on to his earthly ones in his own voice. Sittings with him were friendly, down-to-earth affairs, with none of the dramatics associated with the likes of Helen Duncan. Perhaps that is why people from all across the world sought him out. Best travelled extensively, to Australia, India, even South Africa and counted amongst his clients members of royal families and celebrities. People trusted him and that trust was merited because, whatever secrets Best knew, he took them with him to the grave.

A typical example of his work is that cited by Agnes Kemp Miller, a lifelong devotee of Spiritualism. In an article submitted to the *Ghost Club of Britain* newsletter, Summer 2002, she relates how she was often visited by what she describes as "ghostly presences", from early childhood onwards. She came to realise in time that these spirits were nothing to be afraid of, that they were visitors from the spirit world and intended her no harm. Her accounts of visitations are vivid and often humourous.

But one experience really stuck in her mind. Waking up during the night, she beheld a little boy, about four or five years old, gazing up at her from his perch at the side of her bed.

"He had nice blonde hair and I noticed his bright red jumper. When I put out my hands and asked him what his name was, he giggled childishly and vanished."

The mystery of this little one's identity was resolved by Albert Best, whom Agnes sought out for a private sitting some time afterwards.

Best made contact with Agnes's husband, who had died a few years previously. He informed her that the little boy she saw was her grandson Stephen, whom he had just met on the other side. Stephen had died while still a toddler, and was now growing up in the spirit world. At the time of this sitting, he was four years old, according to Agnes's husband.

Spiritual healing

Best's work was not restricted to passing on messages from the other side. He was also a renowned spiritual healer, and worked for many years at Thornhill, a non-denominational healing centre in the Southside of Glasgow, established by a wealthy businessman who had retired early following a heart attack in 1959.

Just as mediums depend on their spirit guides, so Best the healer relied on the services of his spirit helpers, Dr Wong, Ally and Hans. These helpers provided spiritual support and guidance and sometimes even supplied messages from well-wishers on the other side who wished to reassure the patient.

Best healed by placing his hands on a patient's body, never seeming to penetrate the flesh. It may have been unremarkable to watch, but some of his results were astounding.

Rosalind Cattanach's tribute to Albert Best, entitled *Best of Both Worlds*, relates the story of Morag and James Darroch, of Greenock, whose daughter Janice greatly benefited from her consultations with the Spiritualist healer, beginning in February 1969.

At nine months, she was "literally wasting away. She had no control or power in any of her muscles, and in effect couldn't even suck a bottle." Even the medical specialists were in despair, so the Darrochs took their daughter home, with the object of at least ensuring she was comfortable and in the company of those who loved her.

It is not clear how much faith these two understandably anxious parents had in Spiritualism, but they had nothing to lose after all, and so they called on Albert Best.

Upon meeting the ailing infant and her parents, Best asked James to hold the baby and as he did so, he felt "a very strong heat going through my body and presumably being transmitted to the baby". Whatever was happening, it felt very peaceful and positive.

Afterwards, Best instructed them to feed Janice. They did, without hope initially, and were astonished to see her suck on her bottle with an unprecedented vigour.

Though Janice never thrived, she had a genetic disorder that caused her to be chronically debilitated, her parents are convinced she lived a much longer and happier life than would ever have been possible without the intervention of Best. They had not expected their little daughter to live beyond infancy; in fact, she lived a relatively full and enjoyable life, dying finally in 1991 at the age of 22.

"They've come. You will have to let me go"

But what of Best's own tragic circumstances? He told a reporter for the *Psychic News*, in January 1972, that he had never attempted to contact the long lost Rose himself because, simply, "I don't wish to".

However, he did meet her once, through the agency of a Medium called Alec Martin, of Ayr, at a Home Circle meeting. Martin was a physical medium and brought forth the fully materialised form, not just of Rose, but of her and Albert's three children too. Best embraced them joyously but, as far as all the accounts go, that was the only time he met her again this side of the grave.

Best died on 12th April, 1996, having slipped into a coma over a week before. However, he did wake up just before he died, to see his friends, including the Glasgow medium Gordon Smith, standing round him. Smith, who was greatly inspired by Best and enjoyed a close friendship with him, gradually became aware of another, spiritual presence at Best's bedside but could see no-one else standing there. But when Best, speaking barely above a whisper, announced that "My wife is here and the children",

Smith felt he could "see" a slim young woman with long, reddish-brown hair and a slowly beaming smile.

"They've come. You will have to let me go," were Best's final words on earth.

Though Best was a delightful man to meet, the *Psychic News* reporter was frustrated by the medium's reticence. This trait never deserted him. Years later, he only agreed to Rosalind Cattanach's biography of him if she kept the personal details to a minimum! Perhaps he will be more forthcoming from the other side?

gordon smith

Glasgow born and bred, Gordon Smith is known as the Psychic Barber because he combines a career as a hairdresser with that of a practising medium and is author of two books, *Spirit Messenger* and *The Unbelievable Truth*. He is hailed as "Britain's most accurate medium", counts Professor Archie Roy of Glasgow University, former professional footballer Ally McCoist and the actress Michelle Collins amongst his fans and has a diary booked up months in advance with engagements across the world.

Unlike Albert Best, who served as something of a mentor to this rising talent, Smith is very upfront and at home with the media. Though he would never spill the beans on the experiences of private individuals, he is eager to spread the word about Spiritualist mediumship and to persuade people that there is life after physical death.

Seventh son of a seventh son

Gordon Smith was born the seventh son of a seventh son. To the superstitious, this fact alone already marked him out as someone who would develop supernatural powers. But it was not until adulthood, by which time he was well established in a regular, strictly non-psychic profession, that he was to fully realise those gifts.

However, one incident in childhood should, perhaps, have tipped the young Gordon off.

Interestingly, it happened following a quite serious childhood illness. Some speculate that a close call with death, whether brought about though illness, or working with ailing and dying people, for instance in a hospital, or being around the dead, as during a war, can trigger a powerful reaction in "sensitive" people. Maybe it was Smith's rheumatic fever, so severe it required a spell in hospital, that prompted what came next.

It happened during his period of convalescence, when he was playing in the garden, his pals and brothers having gone back to school for the afternoon. Into his line of vision sauntered a familiar figure, that of Ummy, a local tic-tac man and a firm favourite with the neighbourhood children. Ummy, when he had had a good day at the race track, was in the habit of passing a few pennies their way, and throwing in a few songs and jokes just for good measure.

The only thing odd about Ummy this day was that he was singing a song about being buried in Dalbeth; a song that did not spring from his usual repertoire. Ummy then bid Gordon goodbye and began walking backwards, waving as he went.

The young boy told his mother, who went rather pale and insisted it was all in his mind. Why? Because, as Gordon was soon to learn, Ummy had been dead for a week and laid to rest in, you guessed it, Dalbeth.

However, Smith was unrattled by this encounter. His meeting with the spirit form of Ummy had been a pleasant experience, had seemed utterly natural; there was nothing to be afraid of.

Though his grandmother had reputedly been a woman of psychic powers, Smith's immediate family were not particularly keen to encourage this latent gift of his. Though he had a number of curious brushes with the other side during his young life, all talk of psychic ability was pushed into the background and he left school and entered the world of work with the kind of expectations you would expect of a young man of his age. Starting out as a barber, Smith hoped one day to run his own hairdressing salon and own a big, swanky house in the suburbs. The spirit world, however, appeared to have a quite different career plan mapped out for him.

Gordon Smith, in *Spirit Messenger*, while acknowledging that his parents were less than enthused about his youthful abilities as a psychic, pays homage to them for their hard-working, kind and loving attitude to life – an attitude he has clearly adopted and which has stood him in very good stead throughout his career.

For those with a gift there appears little danger of a psychic ability being snuffed out by a lack of parental encouragement. People with psychic abilities, even those from the most sceptical of families, always seem to get a call from the other side at some point in their adult lives.

As Gordon Smith says: "If the spirit world wants you to work for it, it will make sure you are in the right place at the right time. The chance will never go past you."

Finding spiritualism

It was not until Smith was 25 that he was forcibly reminded of his strange childhood experiences. Waking up one morning, Wednesday March 9, 1987, to be precise, he saw the figure of Brian Peebles, the brother of his hairdresser colleague Christine. By the time Smith was fully awake, Brian had vanished and he concluded it was all just a figment of his half-waking consciousness.

It was no such thing. As Smith heard on the radio an hour or so later, Brian had been killed in a domestic fire leaving his sister absolutely devastated.

Of course, Smith wanted to do all he could to console and help Christine but he admits he was a shade reluctant when she asked him to accompany her to a Spiritualist service at the Glasgow Association of Spiritualists. He felt it was too soon after Brian's death and that meddling with the dead would only rub salt into already raw wounds. But they went anyway, on Christine's insistence.

The service was touching and Christine was rewarded with a message, conveyed via the Edinburgh Medium Mary Duffy, from her late mother. Duffy added that the best man to help Christine through this was a Glasgow Medium called Albert Best, whom she did eventually seek out, four years later, and who helped her make contact with her much mourned brother.

Another important thing happened at the Glasgow Association séance. Duffy paused to remark, to Smith, that his psychic grandmother was present, and like Alec Harris, the Welsh Medium many years before, who encountered his late sister Connie at a séance, was reminded of his gift and told that, one day, he would get around to using it.

Smith took heed and began attending a Development Circle at the Spiritualist church in West Princes Street, in Glasgow's West End. Smith was fortunate because this Circle suited him to a T and he attended for eight years, during which time he went from being a rather baffled, often amused and frequently over-earnest rookie to a true professional with the common touch.

One important lesson he learnt was that you can, in fact, learn too much. Intellectualising the art of mediumship is fine for academics and those, like Helen Duncan's husband Henry, who are fascinated by the gift but do not possess it themselves, but can serve to severely clutter the mind of the practising medium, often to the detriment of their psychic work.

One of Smith's mentors told him to slow down, and let his natural development take its course. And "all of a sudden, spiritual development became fun. Because I stopped trying to be a medium, my natural gift began to resurface".

While it seems that each medium has his or her own way of doing things, that is not quite the whole picture. Most experience the spirit world in a number of different ways, and not always consistently. Albert Best, for instance, usually "heard" his spirits, but the story he told his friend Leonard Goss alerts us to the fact that he had the capability of being a physical medium, though he chose to reject that path.

Gordon Smith often "hears" his spirits, making him a clairaudient. But sometimes he doesn't. Sometimes he "sees" them (clairvoyant) as well, and sometimes he neither sees nor hears them but clearly "senses" them (clairsentient).

Smith puts these differences down to the personality of the spirit form, equating those whose presence is felt rather than heard with quiet, rather reticent personalities who nonetheless want to come forward and make contact with a living friend or loved one. Others, by contrast, are noisy and lively, as they often proved to have been in life.

One young man, Alan, whom Smith contacted on behalf of his mother, had a gregarious personality and that came through to the medium, loud and clear. He rarely got through a sitting without laughing a few times.

The public awaits

Smith's first public demonstration of mediumship occurred four years after he joined the development circle, and quite by accident. Though, he recalls, he did get a slight forewarning. Driving to the Spiritualist service that night, he felt what he describes as an inexplicable upset in his stomach. "It was the same type of sensation that I got just before a psychic experience or premonition."

Pity he hadn't put money on it because, when he got to the church, the booked-in medium had failed to show up and there was no-one else capable of taking the service other than Smith.

Though he was petrified, he found that, once up on stage, his nerves vanished and the spirits were willing. Which just goes to show what any medium worth their salt will tell you; you cannot commune with the spirits through sheer effort of will, it is a question of letting them come to you.

As time went on, Smith became a hugely popular personality on the Spiritualist circuit perhaps because, like Best before him, he works hard to keep the atmosphere light and to reassure those who may be a little spooked by their first encounter with the spirit world.

However, he did find that being psychically sensitive has the potential to affect, to their detriment, other facets of your life. It is quite understandable that, when a medium's faculties are heightened to the extent they need to be to communicate with the dead, those same faculties run the risk of being overwhelmed by ordinary life. Smith certainly found this to be the case. "Everything in your life becomes exaggerated; you begin to see molehills as mountains."

To counter this effect, he has since learnt to take himself off and do wilfully ordinary tasks, such as walking the dog and washing the car, to "ground himself" again.

Another thing he has to guard against, Smith says, it taking his work home with him. If he doesn't "switch off", he could be subject to voices from the other side at any time of the day or night.

"My private life is my private life, and I enjoy some space away from my work at the end of the day. Otherwise, I'd never get any peace!"

Gordon Smith does not prepare for his Spiritualist demonstrations as the best preparation is a clear mind. One meeting, held at a popular Glasgow Spiritualist church, was recorded for a Radio Netherlands broadcast, an indication of how widespread acclaim for Smith has grown.

This was a very successful night, Smith having made contact with five different spirit contacts by the time he got round to Malcolm, a reticent young man sitting huddled near the back and quite obviously trying to avoid being noticed.

Malcolm had attended reluctantly and only at the behest of his sister-in-law who had insisted that his mother, recently deceased, was trying to make contact with him. That, she said, was why the electrics in the house kept going awry; his mother was trying to get his attention!

He was unconvinced and simply sat there, waiting for the ghastly proceedings to be over.

But then Smith's gaze fell upon him. Pointing to "the man with his arms folded, you sir", Smith told Malcolm that "I have a woman with me who is not long in the spirit world".

Malcolm flushed darkly but was genuinely astounded to hear Smith relate details about his mother, and him, that he could not possibly have gleaned from any other source.

Smith concluded with some pretty astonishing proof. He said: "She's been interfering with the electrics in the house. That's just to tell you that she's there with you!"

Sadly, the documentary-maker did not follow up the story to discover whether Malcolm's flickering lights returned to normal thereafter but it is quite clear that, on this occasion, Smith's detailed accuracy thoroughly convinced one very determined sceptic.

A tragic accident

Though he loves to inject a bit of humour into proceedings, some of Smith's experiences have been truly heart-breaking.

One time, a woman called Lee Bright came to him for a private sitting at the well-known Spiritualist church in Glasgow's Berkeley Street. She was grieving for her younger son Alan, who had been killed in a road accident at the age of 28 years.

As is the case with many bereaved mothers, mixed in with her sorrow were flecks of guilt. She felt that, as Alan's mother, she should somehow have always been able to prevent any harm coming to him. Knowing that these guilty pangs were irrational did not help any.

At the sitting, Gordon made an instant connection with Alan and was able to reassure Mrs Bright that it was truly her son's messages that he was conveying. How? Because Gordon was able to relate details, both of the accident and of subsequent activity in the Bright household that proved, to Mrs Bright's mind, that Alan was not only speaking to her, but watching over her. Alan "knew" that his parents had been going through the spare room in their house, which Smith described accurately and in detail, to look through insurance papers, and that they had opened up his wallet to find his credit card, as they had been asked to do.

"This was important to me because both Iain (her older son) and Alan knew they could leave wallets or even letters and diaries lying around and I would not look at them. I have a great belief in one's right to privacy."

At each subsequent sitting, Mrs Bright left with the impression that she had "spent time in Alan's company" as Smith related family legends and in-jokes that only her son could have told him. Surely.

Well, Iain wasn't so sure, but he was persuaded to attend a sitting with his mum and Gordon Smith. That sitting convinced him that life after death was for real, and a considerable weight was taken off his shoulders.

Talking to the dead

As mentioned earlier, Smith is no stranger to media coverage, though he bristles when approached by reporters who have already made up their minds about Spiritualism and mediumship before they have so much as said a single word to him.

This was not the case with regards to *Talking To The Dead*, a balanced BBC series examining the phenomena of the afterlife and communication beyond the grave.

As part of the programme, Smith was filmed holding a sitting with a middle-aged couple, Greta and Andrew, who had lost their son in tragic circumstances.

Unbeknownst to Smith, Greta had actually already had contact with her dead son, through the agency of two different mediums, but on each occasion had left wanting more. She felt that the messages she had so far received were insubstantial and not enough to set her mind at rest.

A grief counsellor, contributing to the programme, warned that Greta would never achieve closure nor come to terms with her loss so long as she believed it was still possible to talk to her son. Greta obviously felt differently; she felt that if she could only be reassured that he was at peace, she could let go.

Smith did make contact with her son and the information he related appeared to be very accurate indeed. He knew not only the boy's full name – and this despite being given no details about the couple, nor asking for any – and occupation, but also a host of little facts and anecdotes that only a family member could have imparted to him. Finally, it seemed that Greta was satisfied and ready to move on.

Vulnerable people

These stories bring home the point that mediums most often deal with people who are in great emotional pain and therefore intensely vulnerable. Opponents of Spiritualism and psychic work in general often point to this as the springboard for their objections. Harry Houdini, for example, believed that mediums were like vultures, preying on the needy and exploiting people's distress.

Supporters of Spiritualism and many "agnostics" counter-argue that mediums, like priests and ministers, provide comfort when it is needed most and far from exploiting people, offer a valuable service.

Though mediums appear to be focussed on the dead, their real concern is with the living people that are left behind. As Gordon Smith told Greta, "You have a life after death and you've got to build on that."

He also makes a point of not charging for private sittings or for the mediumship demonstrations he gives at Spiritual church services. Though he does charge a fee for major public demonstrations, that money is donated to charity. Perhaps the idea of charging for his services is something he finds distasteful, or perhaps he is just taking a leaf out of the great levitator Daniel Dunlas Home's book, who made it a point of principle not to charge for his services either.

Whatever his reasons, Gordon Smith relies on his hairdressing and the proceeds from his two books to get by. His dream of a buying a big suburban house has, apparently, had to be put on hold as the demands of mediumship, particularly when you are as popular as Smith, are incompatible with the extra hours you need to put in to reach the top of the hairdressing profession.

A challenge

Like many mediums, Gordon Smith is adamant he has nothing to hide and when challenged to prove that he is really doing what he says he is, he usually accepts. So when he was asked, in 1994, to give a demonstration of his powers before an audience comprising members of the Scottish Society for Psychical Research, he agreed with no hesitation. Archie E Roy, Professor of Astronomy at the University of Glasgow and a keen student of Spiritualism, was to host the event, with Tricia Robertson, a statistician from the Society in attendance.

He was naturally a little anxious that the spirits might not show. Sometimes they do that, he says. In which cases, he is always frank and honest with his clients; it's that or make something up as he goes along, which he says he would never do. When he draws a blank, he suggests that his client either come back at a later date, because possibly it was the wrong time, too soon maybe, for this particular spirit to speak, or find another medium, who may be more successful in this individual case.

Smith hoped he would not have to convey such a message to the Society members, who were packing out a specially reserved hall at the university on the night in question. The night was a great success though Smith admits he can remember little detail of the actual messages conveyed. This has echoes with Helen Duncan's strange comment to the formerly sceptical Mr Ramsden, to whom she admitted that she had never herself seen the materialisations she conjured out of the air. Though Smith is not a trance medium, in that he does not descend into an altered, somnambulistic state before commencing his dialogue with the dead, he is still a channel for communication rather than the source of it.

At a subsequent meeting with the Society for Psychical Research, Smith was challenged by an audience member who asked him did he not just pick up clues from the way a person behaved, coupling it with information gleaned through telepathy? Smith stated emphatically that he did not, citing research by such eminent bodies as the Society for Psychical Research based in England, whose rigorous study of mediumship is detailed elsewhere in this book. Smith himself has been the subject of a study, conducted by PRISM, the acronym standing for Psychical Research Involving Selected Mediums, which is cited in Tricia Robertson's book *The Truth is in Here*.

The aim of the study was to test the theory that mediums make such general statements that someone, somewhere is going to be able to salvage a comprehensible message out of it, just as a vague horoscope can be stretched to fit anyone's day.

The study was to be conducted using statistical methods, this being Robertson's field of expertise after all. The experiments, which included such rigorous techniques as double-blind testing, requiring the mediums and recipients to sit in separate rooms to rule out the possibility of verbal and non-verbal glues being given, were conducted over a period of four years.

The results were quite astonishing, especially those produced from Gordon Smith, whose average accuracy rate was 98 per cent, quite the highest of all the mediums tested.

Professor Roy said afterwards: "There is no doubt from the work we have done that mediums can obtain information using more than the five normal senses.

"The results so far have been assessed with hard mathematics and statistics. We believe that we have disproved the ideas that all mediums are able to do is make general statements."

Indeed, even opponents to Spiritualism and mediumship admitted, upon closer inspection, that the methodology used in this study were scientifically sound.

Speaking to a newspaper reporter, Gordon Smith said: "A lot of scientists would argue that I am downloading the information from somewhere and I wouldn't argue with that. There's not always a spirit contact. If you were very emotional you'd give off a lot of feeling and I would be able to pick up the fact that you were going through a crisis time."

But that would not be enough to generate messages, accurate

ones, from the other side and in any case, "with a lot the work I've done with Archie Roy I can't even see the audience so I can't fall back on body language".

Revival, and a down-to-earth approach for the 21st century

In the century and a half since Spiritualism was established on any kind of organised basis, its public image has altered dramatically. The days of phantasmagoric materialisations, levitations through open windows and darkly-clad dowagers holding hands in dimly-lit drawing rooms are long gone. These days, a Spiritualist gathering is a breezy, daytime affair with mediums who are matter-of-fact and often gifted with a sense of humour.

The mysterious, amateur dramatics overtones may have gone, but it seems the popular fascination has not.

In recent years, Spiritualism in Scotland has enjoyed a real revival, with attendances at Spiritualist churches and home circles rocketing for the first time since the Second World War.

The Spiritualist National Union now has in the region of 20,000 members in the UK, with three times that number estimated to be regularly attending Britain's 300+ Spiritualist churches.

Why now? World events like the attacks on the World Trade Centre on September 11, 2001, the conflicts in Afghanistan and Iraq, and the rising death toll through drugs, AIDS and cancers will have heightened people's sense of their own mortality. Plus, says John Weir, Scottish SNU chairman, modern people are seeking alternatives to the established churches which often struggle to make sense of a rapidly changing world.

He notes: "There has certainly been an upsurge in interest (in Spiritualism). Young people particularly are looking for something different that is not being given to them elsewhere. Spiritualism is answering a need in the community."

In answer to the sceptics, he says: "The only person who can really know if it is genuine is the one who gets a message, and when that happens it is certainly a wonderful experience and it can be really uplifting for someone going through grief. People are mostly in need of comfort."

And no-one is going to argue with that. However, there is the danger of exploitative mediums, who prey on people's grief. The Fraudulent Mediums Act would not exist if these people did not. To avoid them, genuine mediums offer a few tips. First of all, if you can find one, approach a medium who doesn't make money from what they do, or at least choose one who comes recommended by a credible organisation, such as the SNU. Secondly, be aware of what you hope to achieve. If it is to say goodbye to someone, fine, but don't keep returning, opening up those channels of communication again and again. If you do, you risk never finding the closure you are looking for.

Take it from Gordon Smith, who says: "Consulting a medium should be a spur to allow someone to draw a line under a separation and get on with life. For that reason I rarely give anyone more than one sitting."

GHOSTLY SIGHTINGS AND HAUNTED PLACES

Scotland and Ireland, though relatively small nations, have had more reported sightings of ghosts and phantoms than any other nations on earth.

Scotland has a long tradition of ghost stories, borne of a storytelling heritage, and the very best ones are those that contain a germ of truth, that relate to real places and real encounters.

One theory as to why we are so infested with phantoms and supernatural visitors is that, though our history is no longer than anyone else's, it is a particularly brutal one. And indeed, places like Culloden Battlefield, where scores upon scores of brave Highlanders were savagely butchered like cattle, and Edinburgh's underground vaults, where victims of the Plague lived out their last wretched days behind closed doors, are famous for their ghostly presences and chilling atmosphere.

Castles are equally likely contenders for haunted status because they served not only as family seats, but as fortresses and prisons. Many prisoners were tortured and starved to death within the impenetrably thick walls of Scottish castles, often at the whim of a nobleman who had let power go to his head. Wouldn't you, in such circumstances and given half the chance, come back to haunt your persecutors' ancestors?

Another theory as to why we have such a rich array of ghost stories is that, being the nation that gave birth to the strict Christian doctrine of Presbyterianism, tales of the supernatural provided an outlet for suppressed imaginations. That they were frowned upon and even forbidden only made them the more alluring.

Most ghost stories have something in common with the modern-day urban myth. Namely that they always happened to a friend of a friend of the storyteller, never to him or her directly. And it will invariably have occurred in the very city, town or castle, in which you are listening to it.

Thus the same ghost story crops up again and again, attached to different places and related to different sources. Someone, somewhere, perhaps did see something that made their skin crawl and their throat close in fright, but who they were, and where, inevitably gets lost in the telling.

While most stories of hauntings and phantoms are told for the purposes of entertainment, some people have had terribly frightening experiences at the hands of what they believe to be supernatural forces, and ghost-hunting is a serious business.

Psychologists sometimes argue that ghostly disturbances are the product of a troubled psyche; a theory that is often applied to the phenomenon of poltergeists. But that does not explain why people without personal problems see ghosts, why so many different people see the same one, and why these stories endure for years, even centuries.

poltergeists

Poltergeists are a well-documented phenomenon world-wide. Whether or not they are ghosts as such is a matter of some debate. They are not generally associated with any particular person who has gone into the hereafter. Their activities are generally short-lived, the hauntings of a poltergeist not going on indefinitely. Instead, there is generally a period of some weeks or months when activity is particularly troublesome. After this time, the poltergeist will disappear or at least cease its activities.

Poltergeists are closely associated with adolescents, especially troubled children. The appearance of a poltergeist will often coincide with a time of particular trauma for a teenager in the household, whether the trouble be of a serious nature or the usual adolescent angst.

Andrew Mackie's House

Perhaps the most famous Scottish poltergeist is that which came to haunt the house of Andrew Mackie, a farmer in Ringcroft of Stocking, Kirkcudbrightshire. This story is particularly unusual because it was documented in great detail at the time by a local minister who was very much involved in the whole affair, the

Reverend Andrew Telfair. His report is backed up by the testimony of several witnesses, amongst whom are other members of the clergy.

The story dates back three hundred years to the end of the seventeenth century when, inexplicably, the family of Andrew Mackie began to be tormented by some sort of devilish spirit. The haunting lasted for a period of some three months.

The strange events began one night in February 1695, when Andrew Mackie went out to check on his cattle. When he got to the byre, he found all the beasts running loose. A little puzzled, he tied them up carefully before retiring for the night. Next morning, however, when he went to attend to them, he found that they had become untethered once more. The next night, the same thing happened again. Andrew tied his beasts with even extra care, only to find them let loose, how he knew not, by the next morning. The next morning again he found one of his cattle suspended from the roof of the cow shed by its tether.

One night, a basket full of peat that had been standing outside found its way into the house as the family slept. The basket was upturned, and the peat was piled up in a heap in the middle of the house. Somehow, the peat had been set alight. Fortunately the family was wakened by the smell of smoke and disaster was averted.

The disturbances continued – there then followed a period in the month of March when the house and its occupants were bombarded by stones. Kitchen implements, furniture and bedding were inexplicably moved, turning up in the strangest of places. On one occasion a child of the family was alarmed to see a figure huddled in his blanket in the corner of the room, close to the fire. When someone had plucked up the courage to investigate and pulled the blanket back, it was found that it was not a person under the cover but an upturned stool.

The flying stones became bigger and better in their aim; the members of the family were being knocked and bruised by them and neighbours coming to call were similarly assaulted.

The house was continually disrupted by bangs, knockings, furniture moving and doors slamming. Over time, the family observed that the activities were more frantic on Sundays or at times when the members of the family were praying together.

As the trouble escalated, the family called in Reverend Telfair. He led the family in prayers, but as soon as he left the house, the stone-throwing resumed. Things calmed down in the following few days, but the next Sabbath saw an increase in the stone-throwing. Reverend Telfair offered to spend the night with the family. The spirit rewarded his efforts with more frantic activity. Telfair himself was struck by stones and a stick. Furniture made strange noises; objects flew at people across the room.

As Telfair knelt in prayer, he felt something on his arm and looking down, saw a ghostly white hand at his wrist.

In the following days, the spirit continued to vent its anger. People were hurled across rooms in the house, scratched, had their hair pulled and were beaten with sticks. The stone-throwing continued relentlessly. The children had their covers torn off them as they lay in their beds. Then they were beaten about the hips by an invisible hand.

The spirit began to make itself heard. As the family were praying, they heard a voice saying, 'Whist! Whist!'

The torment continued unabated until April, and the bravery and tenacity of the family must have been considerable, for they remained in the house in spite of it all. In April, Telfair sought the assistance of his fellow clergy, and two ministers, Andrew Ewart and John Murdo, from Kells and Crossmichael respectively, joined the Mackie family in prayer one night. The ministers suffered considerable pains for their efforts; huge stones were flung at them both and they were beaten with sticks. The whole house was in more turmoil than ever. Fires began to break out.

One day, Andrew Mackie's wife was stepping into the yard when she noticed that a stone slab in the doorway was loose. She lifted the slab and found some bones and bloody flesh underneath, wrapped in cloth. She took the bones from the house to the landlord's house, quite some distance away, thinking that the trouble might in some way be associated with the bones. In her absence, the trouble in the house only increased. The children found burning hot stones in their beds. Fireballs flew around. The stone-throwing was worse than ever. Mrs Mackie returned the bones to the house. The Reverend Telfair prayed over the bones and was beaten severely with a stick.

And so it went on. Then something happened that made all concerned wonder whether there was something in the house's past to cause the spiritual disturbances. One day, Andrew Mackie found a note, written in blood, or so it appeared, close to his house.

'3 Years thou shall have to repent a nett it well,' the note read: 'Wo be to thee Scotland Repent and tak warning for the doors of haven ar all Redy bart against thee, I am sent for a warning to thee to flee to God yet troublt shall this man be for twenty days repent repent repent Scotland or else thou shall.'

Was there a connection between the bones and the message? Had there been a murder in the house? The house was not old; it had been built only twenty-eight years before. An investigation into the past history of the building ought not to be difficult. Accordingly, all previous occupants were brought before a committee consisting of Andrew Telfair, the landlord, Charles Maclellan, and others. They were all asked to touch the bones. Nothing untoward occurred, so the committee sent the bones to Kirkcudbright for examination by an assembly of ministers. Five ministers were then dispatched to Andrew Mackie's house to pray. The spirit, angered as ever by religious intrusion, flew into a fury. Stones broke through the roof of the house, and the whole building seemed to shake. Telfair details some of the spirit's activities as follows:

It brake down the barne door and mid-wall and threw stones up the house; But it did no great hurt: it gripped, and handled the legs of some, as with a man's hand; it hoisted up the feet of others while standing on the ground, thus it did to William Lennox of Mill-House, my self and others, in this manner it continued till ten a clock at night.

The ministers persisted for three days, but the spirit would not give in to their prayers. Other people from the district joined in the effort. At one point a neighbour appeared with his dog. The dog had killed a polecat on the way to the Mackie's house and the visitor threw the dead creature in a corner of the room before joining in the prayers. Three more people arrived and were very distressed when the spirit picked up the dead animal and beat them about the heads and bodies with its carcass. One of the visitors felt something like a hand inside his clothes and pockets and became so distraught that he was sick.

The following Sabbath brought even more upset. The spirit whispered and whistled and cried out at the family in prayer. The family and friends and neighbours were injured with stones and sticks. Praying men were lifted off their knees by the unseen force.

Two days later, on 16 April, the Mackie family had had enough. They decided to move out of the house for a while. Five of their neighbours volunteered to stay in the house in the Mackies' absence. Strangely, the trouble in the house stopped and the guests were not bothered by the spirit at all. Outside, however, the cattle were found to have broken loose from their tethers, and some appeared to have been disturbed.

Thinking that things might be improving, some members of the family moved back in after a couple of days. They spent one peaceful night, but in the morning found that the sheep had been tied together in pairs by tethers fashioned from straw that had been taken from the stable. After two reasonably quiet days, the spirit started again, with a vengeance. The beating and stone-throwing began again, and lumps of peat were thrown along with the stones. The spirit whistled and called out, 'Take you that!' as it beat its victims. All present continued with their prayers, but the harder they prayed, the more they suffered.

Andrew Mackie was snatching a few hours of sleep when he was woken by the voice of the spirit: 'Thou shalt be troubled till Tuesday,' it said.

Mackie decided to try to talk to the spirit.

'Who gave thee a commission?' he asked.

'God gave me a commission,' was the reply, 'and I am sent to warn the land to repent, for a judgement is to come if the land do not quickly repent and I will return a hundred times worse upon every family in the land. Praise me and I will whistle to you; worship me and I will trouble you no more.'

Mackie prayed for deliverance from Satan. The spirit's reaction was contemptuous: 'You might as well have said Shadrach, Meshach and Abednego.'

Several people heard the conversation between Andrew Mackie and the spirit. One of the company attempted to intervene, but the spirit would not countenance this, dismissing the man for meddling in other people's business. When the spirit became silent once more, the family was no further forward.

The next day, there were seven fires around the house started by the spirit, and the family and neighbours were kept hard at work all day extinguishing them. The spirit appeared to be frustrated at the success of their efforts and began to tear down one of the house walls. The family was forced to take refuge in a barn. As they tried to get some rest, the spirit raised a great block of wood in the air above the heads of the children. 'If I had a commission I would brain them!' it cried angrily.

The fire-raising and the exhausting task of keeping the fires under control continued all the following day. Mackie was in the barn when the spirit spoke to him again.

'Andrew. Andrew.'

Mackie tried to ignore the voice.

'Speak!' commanded the spirit.

Andrew would not speak.

The spirit spoke again, in a calmer tone: 'Be not troubled. You shall have no more trouble, except some casting of stones upon Tuesday to fulfil the promise.'

Telfair, Maclellan and some others joined the family late that night in the house and stayed there for some hours. Apart from some stone-throwing, all was quiet.

On Tuesday, the day upon which the spirit had said it would stop its troubles, the Mackie family and others gathered in the barn to pray. Mackie was the first to catch sight of a black thing in the corner of the building. The thing grew, and it seemed as if it might fill the whole barn with its presence. It was like a huge, black storm cloud. Chaff and mud flew out of the cloud at the terrified onlookers, who then felt themselves being gripped painfully hard around the arms and bodies by the blackness itself. Then the blackness subsided. Everything returned to normal. A quiet night followed.

On the last Wednesday, 1 May, there was one final fire. A sheep house was destroyed, but neither people nor animals were hurt in any way. The disturbances at Ringcroft of Stocking were finally over, and no one was the wiser as to what had caused them.

There were some theories as to what might have triggered the trouble. Reverend Telfair put three of these forward in his account of the happenings.

Some years before the house was occupied by the Mackie family, it was the home of a man called McNaught. McNaught was a miserable soul. Desperately poor and in frail health, he wondered if some evil force might have taken ill against him. He had sent his son to ask the advice of a spae-wife, or fortune-teller, some distance away. His son had gone to see the woman but had met some soldiers on his way home, enlisted and gone abroad. He finally sent a message back to Ringcroft relating the spae-wife's advice. Under a slab at the threshold of the house could be found a tooth. When the tooth was removed and burnt, good fortune would return to the house. The message got back to Ringcroft too late, however, for Mr McNaught was dead.

The new tenant of the house, a man called Thomas Telfair (no relation of Reverend Telfair), heard of the spae-wife's words, lifted the stone, found a tooth and burned it. He had had no trouble whilst in the house. Perhaps McNaught's misery, Telfair's trouble-free tenancy and Andrew Mackie's troubles were somehow linked.

A second theory concerned the death of a woman of ill-repute whose belongings had been left in the house after she died. Perhaps the Mackies had taken the things for themselves? Mackie denied this strongly, saying that the woman's things, carefully tied in a bundle, had been returned to her nearest and dearest intact.

The third theory was dismissed outright by Telfair, who knew Andrew Mackie to be a good, God-fearing citizen. The theory was that Mackie, when he became a mason, had dedicated his first child to the devil.

The strange occurrences have sparked off many a lively debate in the years that have followed, but no one has come any closer to finding out what it was that tormented the family of Andrew Mackie for three terrible months in 1695. Why it caused so much trouble is just as much of a mystery and will no doubt remain so.

The devil of Glenluce

Forty years before the astonishing catalogue of events at Ringcroft of Stocking, the household of Gilbert Campbell, a weaver in Glenluce, was disrupted by a similar presence. This story is more typical of poltergeist activity than that of Andrew Mackie's house, in that the spirit appeared to be closely connected to the children in the family, in particular to Campbell's son, a young student at Glasgow University.

The first indication of trouble to come was given when Campbell's daughter, Jennet, began to complain of strange noises in her ears. The noises were shrill, like whistling. Then Jennet was heard to utter the words of some unseen spirit: 'I'll cast thee, Jennet, into the well.'

After that, the house was subjected to continual bombardment with stones. Clothing was hurled from drawers, clothes were ripped to shreds, sleepers were woken as the bedclothes were dragged off them by an invisible force.

Much alarmed, Campbell moved his children out of the house for their own safety. The disturbances ceased as soon as the children had gone. The children moved back into the house with the exception of the eldest son, who was studying in Glasgow. For a while things were quiet, but then Campbell's son returned to the house and the trouble started again with renewed vigour. Stones were hurled around, belongings were damaged, and at one point the house caught fire.

The affair caught the attention of the church, and various attempts were made by ministers to exorcise the spirit. The spirit was apparently quite communicative and claimed to have Campbell's son in its power. It claimed to have been sent by Satan from hell to torment the occupants of the house.

While the spirit was willing to communicate with the religious men, it was nevertheless resistant to all their attempts to banish it from the house. It continued to torment the family, beating the children as they lay in their beds, starting fires around the house, hiding the family's belongings or hurling them through the air.

The family showed remarkable courage, remaining in the house throughout all this. Then, without warning, the activities of the malevolent force stopped, and the family was left in peace.

Although no one could be certain as to the cause of the fearful disturbances, one theory connects them to a beggar who had turned up at Campbell's house some time previously. Campbell had sent him away without giving him a penny, and the beggar had angrily threatened to avenge this cold-hearted treatment. It was said that the man was a certain Alexander Agnew, who was eventually accused of crimes against the church and was hanged some miles away in Dumfries. His death apparently coincided with the sudden return to harmony at Campbell's house in Glenluce.

The poltergeist of Sauchie

A much more recent case of poltergeist activity was that which concerned a young girl called Virginia Campbell who lived in the village of Sauchie in Clackmannanshire. The story caused quite a sensation in 1960-61.

The child had moved to Scotland from Ireland with her parents, and by all appearances was a normal, bright little girl. The move to Scotland might have been more traumatic for Virginia than people around her had realised. Perhaps this, along with the fact that she was at a vulnerable age – she was eleven at the time – accounted for the strange occurrences that took place when she was around.

The strange events started in the child's home. Unexplained knocking noises were heard when she was around, and objects, even surprisingly heavy ones, were seen to move. The child herself was very distressed by what was happening. Her mother kept her home from school and called the doctor, who prescribed tranquillisers. Virginia seemed calmer, but the strange things went on happening. The doctor had some idea that what they were witnessing might be poltergeist activity. In order to try to eliminate this possibility, Virginia was sent to stay the night with relatives, but the strange events went with her. She was clearly the focus of some sort of paranormal activity. After a couple of weeks, things began to calm down, and it was decided that she should return to school.

Virginia's mother told teachers at the school that odd things were happening at home. Objects were moving; some were flying through the air. It all seemed too strange to be true, but initial scepticism on the part of the teachers soon disappeared when similar things began to happen around Virginia at school. Her desk rose inches from the floor. Other children in her class noticed objects moving from place to place. Once, a door refused to shut behind her. Heavy furniture could be seen to move. Although the activities were less violent in nature than had been witnessed in Virginia's home, they were still happening.

Over the next few months, it became more and more difficult to safeguard the child from the morbid interest of the press. The stories that were circulated were sometimes only tenuously linked to the facts. Surprisingly, the other children in the school were much less hysterical than outsiders in their reactions to events. They became quite matter-of-fact about the situation; when Virginia was around, sometimes things moved – simple as that.

The strange happenings became less and less frequent over time, and after a few months they had stopped altogether.

ghosts iN the house

It is not only buildings of great history or particular architectural interest that feel the chill of the ghost's presence. Homes all over Scotland, both old and relatively new, are claimed to have been the site of supernatural occurrences. Some of these claims will certainly be fanciful, some will be mere sensationalism, but many are simply too strange to be ignored.

Ballachulish House, Argyll

Ballachulish House has more than one ghost, but one particular tale informs us that a 'living ghost' once made a habit of visiting the place.

The house was at one time occupied by the family of Sir Harold Boulton. Many years before he moved into Ballachulish House, Sir Harold had heard his mother talk of a recurrent dream she had had of visiting a beautiful house set amidst spectacular scenery. In her dreams she had become acquainted with every corner of the place, much as if she had really been there.

Several years later, Mrs Boulton, by then quite elderly, visited

Ballachulish House for the first time before her son and his family had moved in. The house was at that time owned by Lady Beresford. Mrs Boulton found to her great surprise that she already knew the house very well indeed – it was the house with which she had become intimately acquainted in her dreams.

When Mrs Boulton spoke to Lady Beresford about this, giving credence to her story with additional knowledge about structural alterations that had taken place over the years, she was pleased to see that Lady Beresford took her quite seriously. Ballachulish House had been visited several times over the years by the benign spectre of a lady. Now, Lady Beresford was quite convinced that the spectre was in fact the living ghost of Mrs Boulton.

Bruntsfield, Edinburgh

There was, until the beginning of the nineteenth century, a house by Bruntsfield Links, one of great age, having been built in the fourteenth century, and of considerable elegance. In the years leading up to its eventual demolition (after which a school was built on the site), the house was inhabited by Lieutenant-General Robertson of Lawers and his staff. Not long after he had taken up residence in the house, the general received a complaint from one of his servants that he was getting very little sleep on account of a headless woman, carrying a baby, who would appear near the fireplace in his room night after night. The complainant was known to have a tendency to indulge in strong drink whenever given the opportunity, so naturally the general assumed at first that his servant was suffering from alcohol-induced delusions. As time wore on, however, the servant persisted with his complaints and eventually left the house to look for work somewhere else.

The general thereafter had the room in which the servant had slept primarily used for storage. No one went into the room at night, so no more ghosts were seen.

The story might have been completely forgotten about had it not been for the fact that the building was subjected to a demolition order some years later. When the builders began to tear the building down, they lifted the hearth in the servant's old room and found the skeletal remains of a woman and a baby. The woman had had her head severed – a particularly brutal act of violence by any standards. The story goes that she must have been sewing when her killer took her by surprise, for scissors and a needle were found beside the bones of her hands, as if she had been holding them. Who she was and why she was killed so savagely along with her child, nobody will ever know.

Learmonth Gardens, Edinburgh

Learmonth Gardens is a quiet street in the respectable district of Comely Bank in the north of Edinburgh. One of the houses has a disturbing history. In the mid-1930s, the house was occupied by a baronet, Sir Alexander Seton, and his family. The family took a trip to Egypt and brought back a souvenir that they would later regret ever having set eyes upon.

The trip to Egypt incorporated a visit to the Temple of Luxor and in spite of the fact that it was illegal to remove anything from the tombs, Lady Seton picked up a small bone as a memento and brought it back to Scotland with her. The bone was placed in a glass case in the dining room.

The family had hardly settled back into normal life when strange and disturbing things started to happen. Crashing sounds were heard and furniture was found in disarray. Ornaments were found broken in rooms that had been empty. Lady Seton fell suddenly and inexplicably ill with a mystery complaint. Time and time again, the family was disturbed by strange occurrences for which no explanation could be found. Strangest of all was the sighting of a ghostly figure in long robes that appeared in the house to several people, residents and visitors alike. Servants of the family became unnerved and sought employment elsewhere.

At one point Sir Alexander lent the bone to a scientist friend. Strangely, the ghostly figure disappeared from Learmonth Gardens for a while, only to be seen at the home of his friend. The family could no longer ignore the fact that the bone seemed to be responsible for the troubles that had been affecting them. Such a story could not remain a secret within the family for long, of course, and the Edinburgh newspapers were soon full of the news of the 'Curse of the Pharaoh', as they called it.

The bone was returned to Learmonth Gardens, and once more the furniture seemed to take on a life of its own. Sir Alexander himself became ill. Unable to withstand the strain any longer, Sir Alexander eventually surrendered the bone to a priest whom he knew. The bone was exorcised and then burnt. Thankfully, the torment came to an end when the bone was destroyed.

New Lanark, Lanarkshire

New Lanark is a historic village at the edge of the market town of Lanark. It was built in the 1780s by the Glasgow banker and cotton merchant David Dale as a social experiment. Workers in the mills in New Lanark had better working conditions than many of their contemporaries elsewhere, and there was also provision for the education and welfare of their families. The village is now a World Heritage site.

It took thirty years for two people from New Lanark to find out that they had both had the experience of seeing the same ghost when they were children. The two were Mary Graham and her brother Alan who, when they were young, had lived with their parents in a flat above the family shop in New Lanark just after the turn of the nineteenth century.

The first to see the ghost had been Alan. The other members of the family had gone out for a while to visit his grandmother, leaving him alone in the house in bed. He had woken up feeling strangely cold and had seen the figure of a woman at his window. The woman was dressed in Highland clothes and she was knitting. She had walked towards the child and then passed him by, walking right through the closed bedroom door.

Alan had been very frightened by the experience, but his parents had told him quite firmly that it was nothing more than a dream, so no more was said about it.

Some time later, his sister Mary saw an identical figure in the flat. She was older than Alan. When she told her parents about what she had experienced, they admitted that what she had seen was probably a ghost. Mary was instructed that she was not to tell her brother, for he would be frightened and would not sleep at night. Mary's parents believed that the ghost meant no harm and probably had some connection with the shop below the flat, which had been at one time a doctor's surgery. Perhaps the woman had died as a result of, or in spite of, medical treatment she had received there. Perhaps she was the victim of something altogether more suspicious – no one could tell.

The tartan cape that the woman wore was possibly a clue as to where she came from originally. Many of the mill workers in New Lanark had come from the Highlands. Perhaps the ghost had been among those who had come to New Lanark to work.

Mary Graham did as her parents had told her – she never said a word to her brother Alan. It was only when they had both grown up that Alan spoke to her of his own encounter with the mystery woman. Finally, brother and sister discovered that they had both seen the same ghost.

Queens Road, Aberdeen

Many old houses are currently being renovated in preparation for a new lease of life as flats or offices. Once such place was to be found on Queens Road, in the West End of Aberdeen.

At the time of this tale, the finishing touches were being completed, notably the application of floor wax to the central stairs which led from the very top of the house to the basement. Working on the final set of steps, which led to what had been the old cellars, the cleaner noticed a corridor to her left that looked newly overhauled. Exploring further, she became aware of a presence, yet could see noone. She could hear him though, shuffling towards her.

Rushing upstairs in a panic, she was met by a group of workmen who needed no explanation. One of their number had been downstairs earlier and had the exact same experience.

a haunted capital

Edinburgh is a beautiful city, of that there can be no doubt. Dubbed the 'Athens of the North' because of the number of classical style buildings it boasts in its graceful Georgian New Town, it also has a proud and ancient castle and a stunning palace that is still a royal residence. Clustered round the Royal Mile, the street that stretches downhill west to east from Edinburgh Castle to the Palace of Holyroodhouse, are the remains of the Old Town, higgledy-piggledy tenements and closes, along with the Canongate, the Grassmarket and the West Bow, all steeped in history and, so we are told, heavily populated by ghostly presences. Edinburgh has seen it all in its time – conflict and siege, plague and fire, murder, intrigue and witchcraft. Seedy and gruesome characters from the past provide a wealth of great material for tourist guides. It must be a joy to have stories about body-snatchers, witch trials and particularly cruel executions to relate to your audience as you stroll the streets of the city with a crowd of visitors. There is enough to tell based on historical fact alone to keep an audience spellbound, but wise tourist guides will know their ghosts as well. There are plenty of them, after all, and their stories add to the thrill of the place. Visitors to Edinburgh can now choose to scare themselves silly on guided tours that specifically concentrate on the horrors of the past and the ghouls that are said to lurk in their wake.

Ghosts can make good money for the entrepreneur, but their manifestations were first recorded long before ghost tours were even thought of, and some of the stories have been passed down through several generations. How did the stories start? Do the ghosts exist? It is left to the individual to decide, for neither the sceptic nor the believer can prove to each other unequivocally whether or not the ghosts do exist.

Edinburgh's ghosts are not all ancient. Things continue to happen in places in and around the town that cannot be explained. The catalogue of reports of supernatural phenomena continues to grow. What is it all about? Is it all hysteria, sensationalism, superstitious nonsense? Is there a rational explanation for everything? The debate will probably never reach a conclusion. Meanwhile, stories of Edinburgh's ghosts will continue to keep children from sleeping soundly and make people stop in their tracks on dark nights in dim cobbled streets – is there anybody there?

Ann Street – the return of Mr Swan

Ann Street is a particularly beautiful and desirable place to live in the heart of Georgian Edinburgh. At the end of the nineteenth century, one of the houses in the street was home to the Swan family. An uncle of the family was a great traveller, and the family was used to receiving letters from far-flung places describing his latest exploits. The traveller would take off for months at a time but would always keep in touch by mail and would appear from time to time, sometimes without warning, to draw breath between his adventures.

One evening the family was particularly surprised to see Mr Swan appear in their midst. They had expected him to be far away at sea, but they were delighted all the same. They rose to greet him as he strolled in through the front door, but before they had time to make him welcome, Mr Swan merely smiled at them, waved and disappeared. It was the oddest thing. The family was left to ponder the strange occurrence for some weeks until news finally reached them that Mr Swan had drowned when the ship in which he had been travelling to some distant place had sunk. The time of his death coincided with his mysterious appearance in the family home. His 'visit' had apparently been a wish to keep in touch with his nearest and dearest in death just as he had in life.

Mr Swan still returns to his old family home in Ann Street. Far from being a malevolent figure, it is said that he is very much a friendly ghost, popping in to say hello.

Corstorphine Castle – the haunted sycamore tree

Nothing remains of Corstorphine Castle apart from the ancient dovecot that stands near the east end of Dovecot Road in Corstorphine, a suburb on the northwest side of Edinburgh. The castle was destroyed in the eighteenth century. Beside the dovecot once stood an old, gnarled sycamore tree, the last of an avenue of trees that led westwards towards the castle. The tree, diseased and fragile, was carefully preserved as a well-loved historical landmark by the Corstorphine Trust until it finally gave way during a storm on the night of 26 December, 1998. The trunk snapped in two leaving nothing standing but a jagged stump.

The story of the Corstorphine sycamore and the White Lady who haunts it, is familiar to all in the district, young and old alike.

In the seventeenth century, when the castle of Corstorphine was still standing, it was inhabited by the Forrester family, who owned most of the land in the surrounding area. The laird at the time, one James Forrester, was a charismatic man, whose overindulgence in alcohol and whose liking for a pretty face and curving figure were well known but, on the whole, forgiven on account of his great charm.

Laird James became embroiled in a passionate affair with a married woman, Christian Nimmo. The lovers were forced to meet in secret, which must have added both a great deal of excitement and a certain amount of tension to the liaison. One such meeting, in the shadows of the dovecot beside the sycamore tree, was destined to be their final. It began with a passionate embrace and ended in a murder.

When Christian Nimmo arrived at their appointed meeting place, Sir James was not there, but Christian knew his habits all too well and sent one of her servants to the Black Bull Inn nearby to seek him out. The laird was found in the inn, as anticipated, and he finally came to meet her by the sycamore tree. He had been drinking heavily, and Christian Nimmo, angered by his inconsiderate and objectionable behaviour, began to quarrel with him. The dispute swiftly took on frightening proportions until suddenly, seized by a fit of uncontrollable rage, the lady pulled her lover's sword from its scabbard by his side and plunged it into him. She escaped from justice initially but was eventually hunted down and taken to meet her end at the hands of the executioner. Her ghost, dressed all in white, haunts the area around the dovecot still, the bloody sword in her hand giving evidence of the dreadful consequences of her temper.

Edinburgh Castle – phantom musicians

Edinburgh Castle has seen more than its fair share of drama and tragedy over the centuries. No doubt there are more ghostly tales to be told about the fortress that stands so proudly on the rock above the city, but the two most famous stories concern a phantom piper and a (sometimes headless) drummer. Both are fitting tales to tell about Edinburgh Castle – the sound of pipes and drums is inextricably linked with the castle in modern times, for it is the venue of the world-famous Edinburgh Military Tattoo, in which massed bands from regiments all over the world thrill audiences of several hundred a night for three weeks every year.

The phantom piper

Edinburgh Castle has seen many alterations and additions since it first came into being as a fortified stronghold. The oldest surviving building on Castle Rock is St Margaret's Chapel, built in the twelfth century, but over the following centuries walls, ramparts, vaults, batteries and a cluster of buildings with both grand and prosaic functions were added until the whole finally came to resemble the castle as people can see it today, complete with a modern visitor centre.

The story goes that in the course of some of these building works (although no one seems sure of when or for what purpose), workmen came upon the entrance to a tunnel that appeared to be leading down through Castle Rock, underneath the Royal Mile. In order to establish how long the tunnel was and where it went, a piper was dispatched to walk as far as he could, playing his pipes as he went, thereby allowing those who remained above ground to follow the sounds of his music and trace the tunnel's route.

It seemed like a good plan at the time. The piper set off, and the people above waited and listened. The sound of playing bagpipes could be heard, albeit faintly, and the sound was moving down the Royal Mile, much as everybody had expected it would. The people above ground kept listening and following the sound. Suddenly, getting towards halfway down the Royal Mile, the piping stopped. There seems to be no record of anybody having gone to look for the hapless piper; perhaps they were all too scared. Rather than take the investigations any further, it was decided to seal the tunnel once more and forget all about it. To this day, it is said, if you listen hard enough above the sounds of the traffic on the stretch of the Royal Mile that leads from Edinburgh Castle to South Bridge, you might just hear the sound of subterranean bagpipe music, for the ghost of the piper still plays in the tunnel below the street.

The phantom piper at Edinburgh Castle is not unique. Elsewhere in Scotland, according to legend, the sound of ghostly bagpipes can be heard in more than one other place, hidden below the earth at Gight Castle.

The ghostly drummer

The story of the drummer at Edinburgh Castle appears to date from the middle of the seventeenth century. Soldiers were garrisoned at the castle under the command of the governor at the time, Colonel Walter Dundas. One night the sentry on guard duty was startled by the sound of a military drum being played. On looking up, he saw a drummer marching on the battlements, beating out a warning of impending attack. The sentry fired his musket and raised the alarm. When others came to his aid, nothing could be seen or heard of the drummer, and the sentry was locked up, suspected of being under the influence of drink while on duty. On subsequent nights, however, the drummer was seen again by different sentries and was heard playing his drum by the governor of the Castle himself. The drummer was obviously a spectre of some sort, but no one knew why the figure kept appearing.

Perhaps the drummer was trying to tell the occupants of the Castle something. Later that year, when the Castle was besieged by Cromwell's troops, the appearance of the ghostly drummer was perceived, with hindsight, to have been a warning of such an occurrence. To this day, there are claims that the drummer still appears from time to time, disturbing the peace of the night with the noise of his drumbeat. Some say the drummer is headless.

Holyrood Palace – memories of murder

There are two well-known supernatural phenomena associated with the Palace of Holyroodhouse, which graces the foot of the Royal Mile. Both bear relation to Mary Queen of Scots.

The first concerns the Italian, David Rizzio, with whom the young queen formed a close friendship when she arrived in Scotland. Mary's new husband, Lord Darnley, did not approve of the friendship and became increasingly jealous of his wife's closeness to Rizzio. With the support of some of the most powerful of Scotland's nobility, Darnley plotted against Rizzio. One night in 1566, Darnley and some of his co-conspirators burst into Mary's private apartments, grabbed Rizzio and stabbed him brutally and repeatedly. After his death, attempts were made to clean the floor of his bloodstains, but these were unsuccessful. The stains reappeared again and again, no matter how often the floor was scrubbed. They can still, some say, be seen to this day.

Darnley, of course, met an unpleasant end himself when his house at Kirk o' Field was blown up barely a year after the murder of Rizzio. He also left his mark on the Palace of Holyroodhouse, albeit in a less colourful manner than Rizzio. In one of the rooms that Darnley frequented at Holyrood, the apartment where he entertained his visitors, strange shadows have been seen many a time by visitors and staff. It seems as if someone is still there, hovering about the room.

Mary King's Close – victims of the plague

Edinburgh City Chambers, which stand on the Royal Mile, were built in the 1750s. Behind the City Chambers, the ground slopes steeply down towards The Mound and then to Princes Street. At either side of the City Chambers some closes of the Old Town still remain, their buildings clinging precariously to the steep slope. Beneath the City Chambers are the remains of another close, sixty-five yards or so of what was once a bustling, overcrowded street of traders in the early part of the seventeenth century. Hidden from the public eye for many years, the close is now a site for guided tours, which are proving to be popular with residents of the city and visitors alike.

Mary King's Close was particularly badly affected when plague hit Edinburgh in 1645. The plague was a horrifying disease. Scores of people died in the outbreak. Such was its severity that parliament moved from the capital city to Stirling. Attempts to isolate the sick and dying were largely fruitless, hygiene being poor or, some would say, non-existent. In the crammed dirty and rat-infested closes of Edinburgh the infection could spread rapidly. Desperate measures were called for to try to halt the rampaging disease, and one of these measures was to seal off Mary King's Close.

The plague passed, but the close remained sealed up. It would have remained uninhabited for ever, but some forty years later the need for accommodation in the already overpopulated city centre was becoming too pressing to ignore, so the city council gave its permission for the Close to be reopened. Some of the first residents were the family of Thomas Coltheart. Ignoring rumours of ghosts of the plague victims, the members of the family moved their belongings into one of the old houses, but they had hardly settled in before they found themselves regretting their decision. The atmosphere in their new home turned most unpleasant – spine-chillingly so. Then, all at once, a severed head appeared before the family, floating in mid-air. It was a grim, grey-haired, bearded old man – or at least, what was left of him.

This was the first of several apparitions. Over the coming days, the Colthearts were visited by a child's head, a severed arm and headless animals. At first, the family tried to pass these occurrences off as figments of imagination, but then stories began to circulate among other new residents to the close of strange happenings that bore a remarkable similarity to those in the Colthearts' home.

What happened after that is uncertain. Some say that the Colthearts fled in terror. Others say that they commanded the spirits to be at peace and then the family continued to live in the Close without further disturbance.

In later years, Mary King's Close was dreadfully damaged by fire. In 1753, work began on the City Chambers and the close ceased to exist. All the upper storeys and most of the buildings at ground level were demolished. All that remains is the small stretch beneath the offices above. But the ghost stories persist. Visitors and tour guides have heard strange noises, such as the noise of a small child crying. Some people have seen things. Quite a few visitors, unprompted, have spoken of seeing the figure of a little girl in one of the rooms. She is said to be small in stature, and dirty and dishevelled. Pustules, a sign of the plague, have been seen on her face. From time to time visitors who have seen the little girl or heard about her have left toys or sweets for her in a niche in the wall. As well as specific sightings such as this, there have been reports of visitors to Mary King's Close feeling 'cold spots' in certain places. The spectres of the past are still around.

ghostly castles

Scotland is famous the world over for its castles, fortified homes of the great (but not necessarily good) of times gone by. Castles in various states of repair can be found in all parts of the country, from the Borders to the far north. Some are still inhabited; some are looked after by the National Trust for Scotland or Historic Scotland as visitor sites of historical interest; some lie in deserted ruins, inhabited only by the spirits of the dead who haunt them. There can hardly be one of these castles that does not have at least one ghostly story to tell.

Abergeldie Castle

The earliest parts of Abergeldie Castle, which stands barely two miles from the royal family's country home at Balmoral, date from the sixteenth century. The castle has had its fair share of visiting guests over the years, including royalty. It also has an extra, uninvited 'guest', known as French Kate or Kitty Rankie. She was apparently a French woman who was employed in the castle at one time. The unfortunate soul was suspected of practising black magic and was arrested and charged with witchcraft. She was confined in the castle until found guilty. Then she was taken to a neighbouring hill, tied to a stake and burnt for her crimes. Her angry spirit returned to the castle after her death.

Ballindalloch Castle

Ballindalloch Castle in Banffshire has quite a reputation for its ghosts. The castle dates from the sixteenth century and has been inhabited by the same family, the Grants and Macpherson-Grants, throughout its history. It is open to the public for some months of the year, and both the members of the family who live in the castle and members of the visiting public have testified to the presence of more than one ghost.

The Pink Tower, a bedroom in the castle, is the haunt of a beautiful lady dressed in a crinoline. Several visitors have seen her. She is a benign presence, and although those who see her might be startled initially, it soon becomes clear that the ghost means no harm.

The dining room, which was originally the great hall of the castle, has a ghost in the form of a green lady. Nobody knows who she is, but she has been seen on more than one occasion.

There is also a male ghost at Ballindalloch. He is thought to be General James Grant, a member of the family who died in 1806. He is buried close to the estate and is said to return there every night, riding a magnificent white horse. It is as if, even in death, he wishes to keep a proprietorial eye on his home and lands. His ghost also walks around the castle itself, making its way through a passage at the foot of the tower to the wine cellar, which was once upon a time the castle dungeon.

The fourth ghost associated with Ballindalloch has a sad story. Apparently, she was a family member who fell passionately in love, only to be rejected. Unable to accept that she had been spurned, she continued to write to the object of her desires, pleading for his attention. The pathetic vision of the young woman is seen from time to time crossing the old Bridge of Avon on her way to post another letter to her beloved. In more recent years, the old bridge was bypassed by a new one, and workmen engaged in the construction of the new bridge are reported to have seen the figure of the young woman several times.

Braemar Castle

Braemar Castle is still used as a residence by the Farquharson family who have been in possession of the castle since shortly after it was built in the first half of the seventeenth century.

The female ghost that haunts Braemar is thought to be a particularly tragic figure who lost her life through a simple misunderstanding. It is said that over two hundred years ago a young couple came to the castle to spend their wedding night. In those days, of course, respectable young ladies were chaste and remained virgins until their wedding day. Many girls were left in a state of almost total ignorance when it came to sex. The wedding night, therefore, was likely to be approached with quite considerable apprehension, even fear, on the part of the bride. What would be expected of her? Would she make a 'good' wife?

The story goes that the young bride at Braemar woke quite

early on the morning after her wedding night to find that she was alone in the bed. She got up and searched the apartments surrounding the bedroom but could find no sign of her new husband. She became very distressed when she could not find him and at once jumped to the conclusion that, having found her to be an unsatisfactory bed mate the night before, her husband had left her. Overcome with shame and confusion, the distraught young woman flung herself to her death from the window of the bridal room.

The poor girl had been sadly mistaken. Her new husband had not left her but had, instead, gone out hunting at crack of dawn while she was still sleeping.

When the bridegroom returned from his hunting trip and rode back into the castle courtyard, he was greeted with the terrible news that his beautiful young bride was dead. How he must have regretted departing without letting his sweetheart know where he was going!

The ghost of the young bride is said to return to the castle whenever newly-weds come to stay there. Whom does she wish to warn? Does she urge young brides not to jump to hasty conclusions, or does she want to remind the grooms that thoughtless behaviour will only lead to heartache?

Cawdor Castle

Cawdor Castle is the haunt of a female ghost – a woman with no hands. The castle stands a few miles from Nairn. It was built in 1370 and became a seat of the Campbell family around 1510–11. The ghost does not date from the early times but from the first half of the nineteenth century, not long after the head of the family became entitled to call himself Earl of Cawdor. It is thought that the ghost was once the daughter of an Earl of Cawdor who found herself smitten with a young man from a rival family. The Earl of Cawdor discovered the secret romance when he came upon the sweethearts one day in their secret meeting place. The Earl was infuriated by his daughter's treachery. He cut her hands off with his sword so that she might never embrace her lover again.

Craigievar Castle

Craigievar Castle is now a National Trust for Scotland property. It stands near Alford in Aberdeenshire and dates from the early seventeenth century. The castle is home to a number of ghosts, so it is said.

The Blue Room in the tower is reputedly haunted by a member of the Gordon clan who fell from the window there. He was forced to his death at sword-point by 'Red' Sir John Forbes, a man of some notoriety. People have heard the footsteps of the unfortunate Gordon climbing the steps to the Blue Room, as if re-enacting the moments before his death.

One of the other ghosts at Craigievar is said to be very selective in his appearances. It is thought that he is the ghost of a musician, a fiddler who fell into the well at the castle and drowned. He is said to appear only to those who bear the name of Forbes.

Crathes Castle

Crathes Castle, the home of the Burnett family until it became a National Trust for Scotland property, can be found a few miles from the small town of Banchory in the northeast of Scotland. Earliest building work on the castle dates from the middle of the sixteenth century, with additions having been made in the early part of the seventeenth century and in the eighteenth century.

In the oldest part of the castle, the double tower, there is a room known as the Green Lady's Room because of the frequent sightings of such a phenomenon over many years. The identity of the Green Lady is uncertain, although some people believe her to have been one of the family. She has been seen both on her own and with a baby. The existence of such a woman in real time has been borne out by the fact that during restoration work in the building two skeletons were discovered, one of a woman, the other of a baby. It is thought to be most likely that the woman had become pregnant in undesirable circumstances and that someone had taken the decision that it would be most prudent to avoid embarrassment to the family and dispose of both mother and baby. In spite of her remains having been freed from their place of hiding, the Green Lady continues to haunt the tower.

Drumlanrig Castle

Drumlanrig Castle is a handsome edifice in Dumfriesshire, which was built in the seventeenth century for the first Duke of Queensberry, William Douglas. He himself spent very little time at the castle, but his family used the castle as a residence for more than a hundred years, after which it became the property of the Dukes of Buccleuch.

One ghost that haunts Drumlanrig Castle is that of a headless woman – not strictly headless, perhaps, for she does have a head, only it is not attached to her shoulders. She carries it about with her in her hands. It is thought that perhaps she is the ghost of Lady Anne Douglas, but how the ghost came to be decapitated is a mystery.

The other well-known ghost at Drumlanrig is a particularly unusual one – a yellow monkey. This creature, unattractive in appearance and disturbingly large by all accounts, can be seen in one particular room of the castle, which is given the name, in very early castle records, of the Yellow Monkey or Haunted Room. Nobody has any knowledge of where such a beast might have come from or if there ever was such an unusual pet at the castle, but over the years there have been several sightings of the hairy creature.

Dunstaffnage Castle

Dunstaffnage Castle, near Oban in Argyll, dates from the thirteenth century and is now preserved by Historic Scotland. Various ghostly figures have put in appearances here, including one of several green lady ghosts that are said to inhabit various places in Scotland. The Green Lady is thought to be a glaistig, and her appearances, always associated with poltergeist activity around the castle, are thought to be omens of notable occurrences, either good or bad.

Duntulm Castle

Duntulm Castle in the north of the island of Skye now stands in ruins, but its colourful history assures it of the presence of more than one ghost.

One of the ghosts is said to have been the reason why the castle ceased to be used for habitation in the early eighteenth century. The ghost is that of Hugh, Uisdean Gillespie Chleirich, who was the cousin of Donald Gorm Mor, chief of the MacDonalds of Sleat. Donald Gorm Mor was an unpopular and brutal chief and had his fair share of enemies. Hugh was perhaps the most deadly of these enemies and had long plotted to kill Donald Gorm Mor, one such plot being made known to Donald Gorm Mor. There are different versions of the story, so it is not clear exactly how this happened, but Donald, having been informed of his cousin's treachery, set about getting his revenge. He laid siege to Hugh's castle, hoping to starve him out. Hugh escaped, disguised as a woman, but he was soon captured by Donald Gorm Mor's men and taken to Duntulm. There he was locked (one version of the story tells that he was bricked up) in a dungeon. But the confinement of his enemy was not enough to satisfy Donald Gorm Mor's appetite for revenge. He saw to it that Hugh suffered cruelly for his treachery. Hugh's only means of survival in the dungeon were meagre rations of salt meat and salt fish. No water was given to him. Needless to say, he died a slow and painful death from dehydration. His screams were said to haunt the castle continuously after his death, causing great torment to all within.

Another ghost that haunted Duntulm was that of Margaret, a ward of the previous chief, Donald Gorm. After Donald Gorm's death, she was placed, according to his dying wishes, in the care of Donald Gorm Mor until she came of age. When she came of age, she was to marry Donald Gorm Mor or enter a convent. According to one source, Margaret was hopelessly in love with Hugh and devastated by his cruel fate at the hands of Donald Gorm Mor. According to another source, Margaret was cruelly rejected by Donald Gorm Mor, principally because she had only one eye. For whatever reasons, Margaret's life was an unhappy one. She did not marry Donald Gorm Mor and eventually entered a convent, but she died soon afterwards. Her ghost returned to Duntulm and could be heard weeping around the castle for many years after her death.

Donald Gorm Mor himself was also said to haunt Duntulm in the company of two drunken friends. The three ghostly figures proved to be quite a trial for Donald Gorm Mor's successor, his nephew, Donald Gorm Mor Og.

Two more ghosts haunted the castle – those of a tiny heir and his nursemaid. It is said that the baby fell from the nurse's arms out of a window high in the castle and onto rocks below, where he died. The baby's father, enraged with pain and grief, ordered that the nurse be tied up and set adrift in a leaking boat. The cries of the baby and his nurse can still be heard in the ruins of the castle and on the rocks where the poor infant met his death.

Ethie Castle

Ethie Castle, about five miles from the town of Arbroath, is now the home of the Forsyth family. The castle as it stands today dates from the early fifteenth century, but there was undoubtedly another building on the site before the present one was constructed.

Cardinal Beaton, abbot of Arbroath in the fifteenth century, commissioned the building of the present castle, and his ghost is said to haunt the place still. He lived at Ethie for several years, and Marion Ogilvy, his mistress, also lived there.

Cardinal Beaton was a powerful figure in the Catholic church and a fierce persecutor of those of the Protestant faith. He had many enemies. His life came to a violent end in St Andrews on 29 May 1546, when he was brutally murdered by Protestant nobles in the castle there.

The ghost of Cardinal Beaton parades slowly round Ethie Castle, particularly in the area close to his bedchamber. The sound of Cardinal Beaton's footsteps is quite unmistakable – his gouty leg thumps and scrapes as it drags along the passageways behind him.

There was another ghost at Ethie Castle – that of a young child. The child could be heard crying sometimes at night. In addition to this, witnesses had heard what sounded like a wheeled toy being pulled across the floor in one particular room in the castle. Eventually, investigations were carried out to discover the source of the strange sounds. A small skeleton was discovered and, alongside it, the remains of a toy wooden cart. The skeleton was removed from the castle and given a Christian burial. The ghost of the child was no longer heard at Ethie.

Glamis Castle

Glamis Castle, a monstrous edifice with looming towers and a gloomy atmosphere, looks as if it ought to be haunted, and haunted it is, perhaps more so than any other place in Scotland. It is now the family seat of the Bowes-Lyons, Earls of Strathmore. Queen Elizabeth the Queen Mother, then Elizabeth Bowes-Lyon, lived at Glamis as a child, and in 1930, Princess Margaret, sister of Queen Elizabeth II, was born there. The castle, although peaceful now, has a colourful past and from time to time spectres from that past return to haunt the living.

Both a grey lady and a white lady have been seen to wander the castle. The Grey Lady is most frequently seen around the area of the chapel and there seems to be no definite idea as to her identity. The White Lady, who appears very infrequently, is thought to be the ghost of Janet Douglas, who lived in the sixteenth century and was the wife of John, sixth Lord Glamis. John died and Janet remarried, settling with her new husband, Campbell of Skipness, at Glamis. The king at the time, James V, hated the Douglas clan, the powerful family to which Janet belonged. As an act of what only can be construed as pure obsessive hatred, James had Janet captured and imprisoned in Edinburgh Castle on charges of witchcraft and conspiracy to poison the king. Her husband and son were imprisoned along with her. After several years' imprisonment, Janet was burned at the stake on Castle Hill. Her husband died in a bungled attempt to flee from the castle, and her son, Lord Glamis, was kept imprisoned until after the death of James V.

Ghastly stories are also told of what befell the Ogilvie family at Glamis Castle in its early days. The Ogilvies were engaged in a bitter and deadly dispute with the Lindsay family, and one day found themselves having to call upon Lord Glamis for refuge. He duly let them into the castle and hid them, as they thought, safely in a secret chamber within the walls. Unfortunately, the Ogilvies had not chosen as safe a sanctuary as they had hoped. Lord Glamis had no intention of letting them out again, for, like the Lindsays, he too despised them. His treatment of them was, whatever he might have felt for them, grossly barbaric. He locked the door of the secret chamber and turned away, never to return.

The poor members of the Ogilvie family were left to starve to death and rot in their hidden location

Nothing more was known of the fate of the Ogilvies until centuries later when one Earl of Strathmore accidentally happened upon the room in which the Ogilvies had been condemned to live out their last, painful days. It is said that when the Earl opened the door and discovered the rotted, skeletal contents of the hidden chamber, he fainted with horror and disgust.

'Beardie' is another ghost of Glamis, with a story that is also linked to the existence of some sort of hidden chamber. Accounts differ as to exactly who Beardie was. Some say he was the first Lord of Glamis, others that he was in fact the Earl of Crawford. Whichever he was (and still is, by all accounts), the story goes that he was a gambling man with a violent temper. Unable to find anyone to play cards with him late one Saturday night as the sacred Sabbath approached, Beardie announced that he would quite happily play with the devil himself if challenged so to do.

Right on cue, a dark stranger appeared and offered to take Beardie on in a card game. The two men retired to a chamber to play. The servants in the castle were intrigued by the noises of shouting and swearing they could hear coming from the room – it appeared that Beardie was losing and losing badly at that. One servant, unable to contain his curiosity, put his eye to the keyhole only to jump back screaming in pain, having been blinded by a shooting dart of flame.

Beardie emerged from the chamber, raging at the interruption. When he stormed back into the room to continue the game, the stranger had disappeared.

The devil had gone, but he had taken with him the soul of Beardie, which the rash lord had gambled away. It seemed as if Beardie was condemned to play cards for eternity, for after his death, some five years later, the room was in constant turmoil with the sounds of cursing, swearing card-players. The story goes that after some years, the chamber was sealed up in an attempt to stop the activities of the phantom Beardie, but his ghost, a fearsome creature complete with straggly beard, is still said to appear in certain places in the castle from time to time and the sounds of raucous card-playing can still, on occasion, be heard.

The first black ghost in Scotland is said to live in Glamis Castle. He is said to be the spirit of a much abused servant boy and is sometimes seen sitting on a stone seat just outside the Queen Mother's sitting room. Some say the child was ordered to sit there and wait until he was told what to do next. Terrified at the thought of the consequences of disobedience, the little boy did just that, but was forgotten about and left there overnight. Being a very lowly servant, he was poorly clad, especially for the rigours of the Scottish climate, and having been left to sit in a freezing corridor for hours on end, he died from hypothermia.

Other ghosts that have been seen at Glamis Castle include the gruesome apparition of a woman with no tongue, who flits across the grounds with her mouth open and bloody; a dark figure dressed in what appears to be a military coat; and a fleeting figure who is seen in the grounds (albeit briefly, for he runs so fast), known as Jack the Runner. The woman with no tongue is thought to have been witness to some ghastly deed and to have had her tongue cut out to ensure that she kept her silence. Just who the other two might be, nobody knows.

The greatest intrigue at Glamis concerns another secret room story and a monster story. At some time there is supposed to have existed, locked up in a secret chamber somewhere within the walls of Glamis Castle, a monster. Accounts vary as to just who or what the monster is supposed to have been and when it came into being, but all seem to indicate that the monster was in fact a family member. There are theories that the monster was in some way connected to Patrick, third Earl of Strathmore. Those who follow this line of thinking point to a picture of Patrick that hangs in the castle. In the painting, at Earl Patrick's side is an armour-clad figure of unknown identity, which looks as if its arms and body are strangely deformed. The theory does not make a lot of sense, for if the monster was so terrible that it had to be kept hidden away from the outside world under lock and key, why did the Earl of Strathmore have it included in a painting?

Other accounts of the existence of a monster, or at least a grossly deformed human being, suggest that the creature might have been the first son of the eleventh Earl of Strathmore. The twelfth Earl, Thomas, was born in 1822, but records apparently show that another son was born to the eleventh Earl and his wife in 1821, a son who supposedly died just after birth. The story goes that this son did not in fact die but was so horribly deformed that the family had to keep him hidden from public view. The child's younger brothers did not even know of his existence until they came of age, when, as a sort of gruesome rite of passage, they were each allowed to discover the location of the secret room. When they had been taken there, the awful truth was revealed to them. The secret of that hidden chamber was never revealed to any woman apparently, and was known only by three men at any one time. Those who became privy to the secret were said to have been shocked to the core – changed men from that day onwards.

Rumour has it that the monster lived until about 1921 – if he was born in 1821, he reached the age of a hundred, a surprisingly ripe old age for someone to live to at the turn of the nineteenth century. If the monster was born around the time of Patrick, the third Earl, then the theory defies belief.

Tales of the existence of a secret room hidden within the walls of the castle, for whatever purpose, are quite believable, for in places the walls are as much as four metres thick. Visitors to the castle have been known to try to find the location of the room by hanging towels out of the windows of all the rooms that they could find. In theory, the one window without a towel hanging from it would be the window of the secret room.

Some say that the location of the secret room is still known and that still only three people living at any one time are privy to the secret. Whatever the contents of the secret room – monster, monstrous remains or something else – its story has attracted a great deal of interest and much speculation over the years. Visitors to the castle at various times in the past century and before have made claims that their sleep has been disturbed by the most awful sights and sounds. And to this day there is a walkway on the roof, known as the Mad Earl's Walk, which is rumoured to be haunted by terrible noises. Here, it is said, the poor creature, the dreadful, hideous family secret, was taken under cover of darkness for exercise.

Meggernie Castle

The ghost of Meggernie Castle in Perthshire seems quite unperturbed by her unusual appearance and is quite willing, it would appear, not only to appear to the living but also to flirt with them.

The room in the castle where the ghost has been witnessed is now known as the Haunted Room, and on more than one occasion, men who have been sleeping in the room have been woken by the sensation of being kissed on the cheek. Those who see the ghost are said to see either her top half or her bottom half but never both together. The ghost is believed to be that of the wife of one of the chiefs of the Menzies clan. Her husband was profoundly jealous of the attentions that she attracted from other men and was forever accusing her of being unfaithful. His jealousy boiled over into uncontrollable rage one night, and he killed her. In order to dispose of the body, he cut it in half. He buried the top half of his wife in the tower and the bottom half in the churchyard. He then went abroad and on his return claimed that his wife had been with him but had died.

It is said that the bottom half of the unfortunate woman parades around the lower floors of the castle and the grounds outside. The top half, meanwhile, stays upstairs and persists in teasing sleeping guests with ghostly kisses.

Sanquhar Castle

Sanquhar Castle, once home of the Crichtons of Dumfries, stands in ruins now but remains the haunt of the ghost of a man called John Wilson. John Wilson was the innocent party in a dispute that was going on in the late 1590s between Sir Thomas Kirkpatrick, John's master, and Douglas of Drumlanrig, ally of Robert Crichton, Lord of Sanquhar and Sheriff of Nithsdale. As an act of sheer spite against Wilson's master, Crichton had John Wilson locked up in jail, falsely accused of certain crimes. When Sir Thomas Kirkpatrick tried to protest Wilson's innocence, Crichton retaliated by having Wilson hanged. Wilson's ghost, groaning and rattling its chains, haunts the ruins of Sanquhar Castle as a testament of its one-time owner's barbarism and cruelty.

A second, female ghost is also said to haunt Sanquhar. She is a white lady, with long, pale tresses, quite beautiful to behold, so they say. Nobody is certain as to the identity of the White Lady, although she is possibly the ghost of Marion of Dalpeddar, who disappeared suspiciously in the 1590s and was thought perhaps to have befallen an unfortunate fate at the hands of Robert Crichton. In the 1870s, excavations around the castle uncovered the remains of a woman buried in a pit. The skeleton still had some hair attached to the skull. The hair was long and blond. Was this the skeleton of the White Lady of Sanquhar Castle?

Spedlins Tower

Spedlins Tower in Dumfriesshire was once upon a time haunted by a particularly hungry ghost.

At the end of the seventeenth century, Spedlins was the property of Sir Alexander Jardine, brother-in-law of the first Duke of Queensberry, William Douglas.

One of the laird's tenants, a miller by the name of Dunty Porteous, fell out of favour with his master. The laird, having right of pit and gallows, apprehended Porteous and took him to Spedlins. Porteous was locked in the dungeon of the tower to await judgment and suitable punishment for his misdemeanours. It was a grim place to sit and ponder one's fate – an underground pit with no light source. The only access to the dungeon was through a trapdoor. No sooner had Dunty Porteous been put away than Sir Alexander had to leave Spedlins to attend to some business in the capital city. He would have to deal with Dunty on his return.

Unfortunately, when the laird set off for Edinburgh, he took the key of the dungeon with him. In his absence, it would appear that either Dunty was forgotten about or nobody thought to break down the door of the dungeon and come to his aid. Whatever was the case, Dunty was abandoned, with tragic consequences.

Some time later, when Sir Alexander finally returned to Spedlins and the dungeon was unlocked, Dunty was found to have died of starvation. It is said that in the agonies of his dreadful hunger, the poor prisoner had chewed at his own hands. Any regret that Sir Alexander felt for what had happened was clearly not great enough, for as soon as the spirit of Dunty Porteous was released from the confines of the dreadful dungeon it started to run riot at Spedlins.

Dunty's ghost was persistent and troublesome, running through Spedlins Tower screaming out in pain and hunger, crying for mercy and food. The spirit would give no peace to the Jardine family. Eventually, a chaplain was summoned to try to exorcise the ghost. His efforts were not entirely successful, for the ghost would not go away. Nevertheless, after a concerted effort, the minister and the family were able to confine Dunty's raging spirit to the dungeon with the help of a bible that was left at the site.

In time the binding of the bible became worn and needed to be repaired, so it was sent to Edinburgh to be rebound. No sooner had the bible left the premises than Dunty's ghost was on the loose again, tormenting the laird and his family as before. The bible had to be repaired and returned with all possible haste in order to confine the ghost once again.

The Jardine family eventually moved from Spedlins. The ghost of Dunty followed them, but the bible was moved too and Dunty remained subdued.

Tioram Castle

Tioram Castle has been uninhabited for more than two centuries, but the ruins that remain are sufficient to indicate to the visitor that it was indeed an impressive sight in its heyday, standing in spectacular surroundings, high on a rock overlooking the sea in north Argyll. It was a seat of the MacDonalds of Clanranald and had a colourful warfaring history.

The twelfth chief of Clanranald was John, who succeeded to his title in the late 1670s. He was a violent man, given to outbursts of temper with a distinctly sadistic touch, by all accounts. It is John, rather than his ancestral home, with which this story is concerned, for it was the man rather than his castle that was haunted. Perhaps it was because of all the wrongs he had done, which was certainly what most people suspected, but the reason does not really matter. John was haunted, not by a green lady or the spectre of one of the victims of his many cruelties. He was haunted by a frog – a hideous black creature of demonic proportions.

It is remarkable how close this story comes to the fairy tale of the princess and the frog. Just as the princess in the fairy tale was pursued relentlessly by her frog, so John found that he was unable to shake off his own slimy follower. If he left it locked in a room, it found its way out and appeared beside him again. If he tried to ride away, the frog would appear alongside him in the saddle. The frog was always there, whatever he was doing, whether he was asleep or awake. On one occasion, John tried to sail away from the castle, only to find the frog swimming alongside the boat. When he refused to let the frog on board, the weather turned so bad that all the people in the boat thought they might drown. John reluctantly let the frog on to the boat, whereupon, it is said, the weather turned calm once more almost instantly.

Perhaps if John had kissed the frog, as the princess in the fairy tale did, he might have found that it turned into something altogether more desirable, but he did not and his frog did not turn into anything else. The hideous creature remained with him, a constant but unwelcome companion, to the end of his days.

Other haunted castles

The stories of the castles in this chapter are just a taste of the hundreds of stories that the ancient fortifications of Scotland have to tell. They are some of the better known ones, but they are not necessarily the most intriguing to the eager ghost-hunter and others with interests in all things supernatural. Other castles that are said to be haunted make a long list indeed, but among them are the following:

Ardvreck Castle – the ghost of a former Lady of Ardvreck.

Balcomie Castle – the ghost of a young boy locked in a dungeon and starved to death.

Balgonie Castle in Fife – Green Jeannie.

Barcaldine Castle – a pair of Campbell brothers.

Bedlay Castle, Chryston – Bishop Cameron.

Borthwick Castle – the ghost of Mary Queen of Scots and the ghost of a young girl impregnated and then murdered by Lord Borthwick.

Brodick Castle – the ghost of an unknown man and a deer.

Buchanan Castle – anonymous groans.

Buckholme Tower, Galashiels – Laird Pringle.

Careston Castle, Brechin, Angus – haunted by the spirit of Jock Barefoot

Claypotts Castle – on 29 May every year, it is said that a white lady appears at an upstairs window.

Comlongon Castle, Dumfriesshire – a green lady ghost

Cortachy Castle, Angus – phantom drummer,

Craigcrook Castle, Edinburgh – said to be haunted by Lord Jeffrey

Culzean Castle – a ghostly piper and a woman in a ball gown.

Delgatie Castle – a female with red hair.

Duchal Castle – the ghost of an excommunicated monk.

Duns Castle – the ghost of a young soldier.

Duntrune Castle, Argyll – the pipes of Coll Ciotach, an Irishman who came to fight he Campbells.

Fyvie Castle, Aberdeenshire – was once the haunt of a green lady

Gight Castle, Aberdeenshire – a ghostly piper.

Inverary Castle – the ghost of a murdered servant boy.

Hermitage Castle, Hawick – haunted by Sir Alexander Ramsay, Sheriff of Teviotdale, and Lord Soulis – 'Bad Lord Soulis' or 'Terrible William'.

Kellie Castle – the ghost of Anne Erskine, who fell from an upper storey window.

Linlithgow Palace – said to be haunted by the ghost of James V's wife, Mary of Guise. The ghost is seen in Queen Margaret's bower

Mcgginch Castle – the ghosts of two chattering old ladies.

Castle of Mey, at one time the Highland home of Her Royal Majesty Queen Elizabeth the Queen Mother is haunted by a green lady.

Muchalls Castle, Stonehaven – had a tunnel that was a godsend to smugglers. The ghost of a young woman of the Muchalls family who went to meet her lover at this tunnel and perished when she fell into the sea.

Neidpath Castle – a white lady.

Newark Castle – the ghosts of women and children slaughtered by Covenanting forces.

Newton Castle, Blairgowrie – haunted by the ghost of 'Lady Jean'.

Skibo Castle – the ghost of a girl lured to the castle by a servant and murdered by him.

Wemyss Castle – a green lady.

exorcisms anð cLeariNgs

To rid yourself of a ghost or malevolent spirit, many have had recourse to exorcism or clearings.

The Church and exorcism

Though most church ministers scoff at the idea of exorcism and houses or people being in the grip of troubled spirits, others are more open to the idea. If nothing else, they see no harm in saying prayers at a person's home if doing so will give them some comfort and reassurance.

The Reverend Charles Robertson, the minister of Canongate Kirk in Edinburgh, is one such. He shrugs off the tale, cited in Roddy Martine's *Supernatural Scotland*, detailing how he led a prayer service of commendation and blessing to rid a young family of a seemingly evil cloud that hung over the baby's cot, as "just a daft story", but it is intriguing nonetheless.

The young couple in question had an infant baby with whom they were naturally delighted. However the mother, Chrissie, became very disturbed by a small white cloud that seemed to hover over her child whenever it was left alone. Upon investigation, it seemed that the cloud was the spirit of a long-dead baby who had been born out of wedlock at a time when such occurrences meant social ostracism and often destitution, and was subsequently murdered by its frightened parents.

What the spirit wanted no-one really knew, though one ghastly conjecture was that it sought a new body to live in and Chrissie's child was the first baby it had come across.

After the Rev Robertson's little service, the cloud never again reappeared and hopefully that tragic baby's soul was thus laid to rest.

Sinister as this story sounds, Robertson believes it is important to distinguish between the idea of exorcism as a rite established to cast out demons and Satanic influences, and simple prayers to rid people of seemingly supernatural activities that trouble them, such as poltergeist-like activity, or inexplicable presences.

These latter, he says, potentially fall into the bracket of a minister's pastoral care.

The Church of Scotland seems to agree. A Deliverance Group was set up in March 2003, to consider the case for deliverance and exorcism. In December the following year, it concluded that though religious rituals could be effective in easing people's fears, an established ritual for exorcism "would do more harm than good and create unwarranted publicity and demand."

Yes, demand. It should be remembered that, following the release of the film The Exorcist, there was a wave of exorcisms and illicit rites, some conducted by ordained ministers but others conducted by occultists and fraudsters. In the UK in 1974, two Charismatic Methodist ministers were involved in a horrendous case that quite rightly made most church people want to steer clear of this kind of activity forever. They had performed an extended, rather harrowing exorcism ritual within the church walls, on a man convinced he was demonically possessed. They then left him alone, thinking he was asleep, exhausted. He woke, went home and, convinced his wife was the devil, bit off her tongue, causing her to bleed to death.

Whilst deliberating the deliverance issue, the church had been warned by mental health experts against encouraging a belief in demonic possession which they believe only further stigmatises people with mental health problems.

Yet, according to a survey of more than 1000 church officials, including prison and hospital chaplains, more than two thirds believe "supernatural forces of evil exist today".

Exorcisms have been carried out, not just by Church of Scotland ministers but also by ministers from the Scottish Episcopal Church and the Roman Catholic Church, though it is only the latter that has a specific rite. This rite, it should be said, is one that most priests "wouldn't touch with a barge-pole" according to one Catholic commentator.

A confused ghost

A particularly fascinating story from the casebook of Albert Best is cited by Archie E Roy, professor of Astronomy at the University of Glasgow and a staunch believer in Spritualism, in his book *A Sense of Something Strange*.

The case concerns a young couple called Karen and Peter Wood, who had two young daughters and had recently moved into a brand new council house in a small town in the West of Scotland.

The disturbances began with mysterious footsteps heard in the corridor. At first, they assumed it was their three year old Katie, but further investigation revealed she was fast asleep in her cot almost every time. Even visitors were aware of the noise, asking Karen if there were other children staying with them.

All this was unsettling enough, but a very frightening incident one night convinced Karen that doing nothing was not an option. Having fallen asleep in front of the TV one evening – Peter was away on business – Karen woke and became immediately aware that she was not alone. Looking up, she saw the figure of a woman, dressed in black, glaring down at her from her standpoint beside the fireplace. She was not a comfortable presence and Karen turned and fled upstairs.

As if that was not enough, a while later, Katie came charging into her parents' bedroom crying that a "monster" had attacked her. They told her it was just a bad dream, but the Woods were worried.

Professor Roy was alerted to the case and he decided to enlist the services of Albert Best, whom he considered to be a very gifted psychic. On the drive there however, he told Best nothing of the circumstances of the trouble, thinking it more appropriate that his friend approach the subject with a clear mind.

Best began by wandering through the rooms of the house, finally stopping in the corridor to observe, "There are children here. They come from the other side. They like to come here. It's a good loving atmosphere so they like to come and play here."

But then he went downstairs to the living room and the first thing that caught his attention was the fireplace; the very spot where the mysterious, malignant ghost had stood. Though the house was recently built, the fireplace had been constructed, by Peter and his father-in-law, from old stones taken from the ruins of a demolished dwelling in an old street on the edge of town. And it was these stones that were, it seemed, at the heart of the problem.

Without being told, Best knew the name of the street they came from – Baird Street – and that the big stone over the fire had been the lintel of the cottage in which the ghost woman had lived in. Best made contact with the spirit, and found that she was as shocked as everyone else to suddenly find herself transplanted to a new house full of noisy kids and her apparent unpleasantness had all been down to her deep confusion and sense of being invaded.

Best discovered that this poor spirit did not realise she was even dead. She apologised for the anxiety she had caused and Best assisted her in "moving on" to the other side.

Walking into the light

Psychics often describe this process as showing spirits, who have become temporarily trapped between this life and the next, how to "walk into the light". Once they do so, they find peace – as do the people they leave behind.

This gentle and compassionate guiding of spirits is a world away from the often violent, frequently hysterical image that most of us have of an exorcism but experience shows that Albert Best's practice is nearer the norm when it comes to dealing with troublesome spirits trapped between heaven and earth.

Looking through the annals of supernatural Scotland, cases of exorcisms are few and far between but that is to be expected. Our modern churches are a little wary of discussing exorcism, viewing it as a rite that belongs in the Dark Ages. Nevertheless, there have been times when such services are called for.

The people through the wall

Lorraine Hedges, a computer programmer lived in a little town called Lilliesleaf, in the Scottish Borders. Being a very pragmatic, down-to-earth sort of person, Lorraine was extremely disconcerted to discover that she and her daughter Katherine were not alone in their own home. And that their "visitors" were varied, numerous and clearly not of this world.

Lorraine described being woken up by something or someone during the night and realising that there were people in her bedroom, usually standing in a corner, looking at her.

At first, she took it in her stride because "they seemed a nice sort of people, there was a mother and a child and they were nice friendly people".

They only stayed for a very short time. "(Then) they would

come towards me but not in a threatening way and they would fly over my head and into the walls. And this went on for ages and I kept on thinking, am I seeing things? What's going on?"

Young Katherine was haunted by spirits too. One time, she returned to her bedroom to find that some mischievous person unknown had splattered bubble bath and body spray, which had been sitting sealed on a shelf, all across her bed. All of which was very tiresome for the sleepless two but not, as yet, actually frightening.

Then things turned nasty. One night, waking as usual, Lorraine felt a presence in the room, a rather malignant presence.

"He was a really threatening man, horribly unshaven. I just got the shock of my life. I really thought it was a real person who had broken in and that my number was up. And then it came towards me and I couldn't move. He went over me and through the wall. I was absolutely petrified. It was the first time I had been frightened; up till then, I'd just accepted it."

No more. The next day, she went through her house with a Native American "Smudge Stick", reputed to have powers to ward off evil. But just to make sure, she also enlisted the services of a Church of Scotland minister, who arrived with a small group of colleagues, and sat in her living room to recite a short series of prayers.

After that, the visits ceased. Not immediately, but over the course of a few days. It was a similar story with the Woods, who had a few more noisy nights, though the noise was increasingly short-lived, and then peace.

Tolbooth Theatre, Stirling

In the case of the Tolbooth Theatre in Stirling, which became the locus for some pretty bizarre goings-on following renovation work, the church was by-passed in favour of a psychic who, according to the theatre's Operations Assistant James Wigglesworth, "instantly pinpointed the exact spot as a place of ghostly activity".

The exact spot being what was once the condemned cell of this former prison. Employees heard what sounded like bodies being dragged across the floor of this cell, and were spooked by the sight of wineglasses flying off tables in the new restaurant and door handles moving by themselves.

Was this a case of an old building still traumatised by its violent past? Or a just a bad dose of mass hysteria amongst its employees?

Well, perhaps the fate of Allan Mair will help to answer this. Mair was a notorious murderer who was hanged outside the Tolbooth in 1843 for bludgeoning his wife to death with a stick. During the renovations, his skeleton was found in a rough wooden coffin, his boots still clearly discernable. After he was removed and given a Christian burial, the disturbances died down considerably.

Galdenoch Tower, Galloway

Galdenoch Tower dates from the sixteenth century. It was originally owned by nobility but after one hundred years or so it changed hands and became part of a farm.

The farmer's family at Galdenoch found themselves in the midst of the struggles of the Covenanters. The farmer was a staunch Presbyterian and proud to have a son who took up the cause against the Royalists.

The Covenanter forces were losing the struggle, and the son found himself on the run, hounded by Royalist troops. Taking a chance that he would find an ally therein, he knocked at the door of an isolated farm one night and asked for shelter. The owner was initially hospitable, but after some time his attitude became more menacing. When the young Covenanter decided that it would be prudent to try to leave, his host attempted to prevent his departure by force. Terrified at the prospect of being handed over to the Royalist troops, the young man fought with his captor and killed him. He then fled for his life, back to Galdenoch. No one had seen him arriving or leaving the farmhouse, so he hoped that the dreadful secret of what he had done would never be discovered.

The young man's crime did go unpunished by law, but he had not seen the end of the man whom he had killed. At Galdenoch a few nights later, the young man was roused from sleep by the ghost of his victim. The ghost made further sleep impossible for the young man by throwing objects and furniture around the room, and laughing and shrieking maniacally. The ghost then set about tormenting the rest of the family, and soon all the inhabitants of the farm spent their days in dread and their nights in fear. For weeks on end the activities of the murdered man's spirit continued relentlessly. A minister was summoned to help, and he tried to exorcise the ghost, but the ghost was having none of it. The torment went on, night after night, week after week, until, driven to distraction, the family fled.

The ghost remained at Galdenoch, and when a new family moved in it started a campaign of mischief of another sort. For most of the time it was quiet, but then, unexpectedly, it would play sudden and dangerous tricks.

The family, sitting by the fire one night, were startled into frantic activity when a peat from the fire suddenly flew out of the hearth. Within moments, one of the outbuildings in the farm was ablaze.

On another occasion the malicious ghost lifted the grandmother of the family from her chair, carried her to a nearby stream, ducked her in the freezing water, lifted her out again and left her on a nearby wall, wet, shivering and frightened half to death.

Many attempts were made with the help of various members of the clergy to rid the tower of its unwanted inhabitant, but the ghost seemed to have the measure of anyone who came. It would taunt people with its demonic voice and laugh at their feeble attempts to banish it.

Finally, one particularly determined minister came to the house. Summoning a band of followers with good, strong voices, he took on the full force of the ghost. The minister and his helpers opened their psalm books and began to sing with gusto.

The ghost was stirred into activity by the sound of the singing and, rising to the challenge, began to sing its own songs in response, louder than the minister's choir. So the minister urged his people to sing louder as well. The louder the choir sang, the louder the ghost sang, until both parties were singing at top volume.

All night the minister urged his choir on as they worked their way through psalm after psalm. When all the psalms that they knew had been sung, they started with the first one again. The people in the choir were very tired and their voices were croaking, but still the minister urged them on, his voice rising above the others as he sought to outdo the ghost. As the first light of dawn glimmered in the distance, the ghost had to admit defeat. Finally, it had found a force stronger than it was. Its creaky voice was heard for the last time as it told the assembled crowd that it had given up.

The minister and his victorious forces, exhausted, made their way home. The ghost of Galdenoch was never seen again.

earth energies

One of the features that attracts so many people to Scotland is its palpable sense of history. Not just the history of clans and kings and bloody border feuds, but also that of ancient times, of druids and wandering Celtic tribes. A history marked by standing stones and ancient burial sites, but whose inner secrets remain tantalisingly beyond our reach.

Despite enormous research, we still know very little about our ancient ancestors, their origins, belief systems and ways of life.

But modern-day investigators believe they have tapped into a least one of the mysteries of our pre-Christian forebears: their knowledge and exploitation of earth energies, those little-understood power currents that criss-cross the landscape, meeting at points that anecdotal evidence suggests are particularly auspicious for rituals, magic and paranormal activity. These points are often notable for their powerful electromagnetic fields, and include standing stone circles, cairns, fairy glens and places that were later adopted by Christians as their own, such as the island of Iona.

Investigators of ley lines often find that, as they attempt to link up one ancient site with another using straight lines, they encounter other curious features along the way. One example, discovered by author and ley line authority David R Cowan, being the "Praying Hands of Mary", a prominent split rock in Glen Lyon on a key point of a ley line that ultimately connects an ancient stone circle at Fortingall, the Croftmoraig Stone Circle in Tayside and Meggernie Castle, famously haunted by the ghost of a half woman, finally finding its source in Staffa, a volcanic island with magical associations linking it, under the sea, to Skye and the Giant's Causeway in Northern Ireland.

For many years, however, study into this area was written off by the scientific community as the pursuit of cranks. But these days, the study of ley lines has gained a newfound respectability as the correlation between electromagnetic fields, some man-made, others not, and human health has become a hot topic for scientific research.

Which suggests that the ancients may well have known what they were about after all, and that it is to our detriment that much of their wisdom has been lost over the centuries.

Ley LiNes

Ley lines are straight tracks or paths which connect ancient and sacred sites. It makes sense that ancient nomadic tribes created these to navigate their way across often treacherous country and straight lines represent the quickest, and therefore often safest, routes.

Ley lines only really became a subject of widespread interest relatively recently, thanks to a retired antiquarian called Alfred Watkins, who got to grips with the subject in the 1920s.

In 1925, he published The Old Straight Track, in which he expounded his theory of ley lines, claiming they were created in accordance with the positions of the sun and moon at various times of the year, particularly the solstices of midwinter and midsummer. He believed that prehistoric ley hunters explored the countryside, seeking spots where earth energies were at their most powerful, the information then being used to pinpoint ideal locations for burial and worship sites.

Though Watkins concentrated on the ley lines of England, subsequent studies have revealed that Scotland is criss-crossed by similar straight tracks. Notable is the one that runs from the ancient city of Stirling to the mystical island of Iona. The latter part of this route actually coincides with the Old Straight Track, a road used by the monks making their way to the ancient island abbey.

However, the earlier part of this track traverses rather less congenial terrain, including the summit of The Cobbler, a notorious mountain in winter, and several major water sources. Thus, unless our ancestors were able to fly, we can only conclude that not all ley lines were transport routes. Perhaps, when thinking in terms of human movement, we should view ley lines as navigational devices, a way of staying on course when maps and navigational instruments were primitive and dangers, from wild animals, weather and hunger, were many.

But ley lines are not just roads. They were, it is claimed, created in order to concentrate and redirect earth energies, to the advantage of those who knew how to use them. Some believe that the points at which ley lines cross have a profound effect on the consciousness of those who gather there, causing an uplifting, even euphoric feeling.

How do they work?

Though we can posit quite credible-sounding theories relating to ley lines' navigational purpose, we really have to rely on guesswork when it comes to their mystical purpose.

One theory has it that ley lines connect ancient power sources and indeed, these tracks often seem to begin, end or cross at such intriguing locations as Maeshowe, the prehistoric burial chambers in Orkney, and Rosslyn Chapel, connected to Glastonbury by a major ley line and widely hailed as the final location of the Holy Grail.

Standing stones and other megalithic structures are said to emit what is called Telluric energy.

Geologists have studied, not ley lines as such, but geological faults which, as it happens, often coincide with ley lines, the most famous example being the Highland Boundary Fault Line.

Geologists believe that the energy created at such places is a spin torsion field, caused by the rotation of the sun and moon interacting with that of the earth.

Another theory is that ley lines were created in order to channel energy to burial grounds. For the Celts, it seems that life was viewed not as finite and linear but as infinite, existing on a sort of endless loop or wheel. The dead went onto another life and it was the duty of the living to ensure they got there, presumably by placing their earthly remains in spots where supernatural energy appeared strongest and which perhaps served as a link between the here and the hereafter.

rosslyn chapel

Rosslyn Chapel, which lies to the south of Edinburgh, is believed to sit where two ley lines cross and indeed, even to this day, it is believed to be a source of tremendous supernatural power. Some even posit the theory that it serves as a kind of portal to another world.

The gothic church was begun in 1445 by Sir William Sinclair, one of the once powerful Knights Templar who fought in the Crusades. He personally oversaw the design of the intricate carvings that were created to form what has been called a "book in stone".

Many believe these carvings contain a code that once cracked could unlock the secrets hidden by the Knights Templar more than five centuries ago.

These secrets, some say, include the whereabouts of the treasures they took from the Jerusalem Temple as they fled the Romans, these treasures including the cup of the Holy Grail and even the mummified head of Christ.

The chapel, which in detail is extraordinarily ornate for its period of construction, is privately owned and the owners have been under intense pressure to allow excavations. So far, they have resisted, perhaps to preserve the mystery, or perhaps because they fear upsetting such ancient secrets.

However, ground-breaking radar revealed, in recent years, the presence of an astonishing structure beneath the chapel – a massive subterranean chamber. Not only did this deep vault dwarf the chapel above but it appeared to have no discernable entrance or exit.

Theories relating to this include one suggesting that the chapel is a kind of spaceship, built on the spot where another one landed in ancient times.

One expert on the chapel and a grand master of the Knights Templar to boot, John Ritchie, is sceptical of the spacecraft theory but believes Rosslyn is more than a repository of looted holy relics. Pointing to the Apprentice Pillar, created by an apprentice who was then murdered by his jealous master-mason, he describes its carvings as representing the Norse Tree of Life, around which vines twine.

"They are in the shape of the double helix, what we now know represents DNA. I believe the chapel itself is the Holy Grail in that it contains the knowledge of life itself, and the rebirth of life."

Certainly Rosslyn, in accordance with much ley line theory, has had its fair share of hauntings, not least by the spirit of the unfortunate apprentice, who returns to weep beside his beautiful handiwork.

Another familiar figure is that of a grey-clad monk who appears both within and without the chapel from time to time.

iona

Iona, situated off the West coast of Scotland, near the much larger and more populous island of Mull, is a tiny island with a seemingly disproportionate and international reputation for being sacred.

It is an undeniably beautiful place, but what drew Columba, traditionally regarded as the founder of Scottish Christianity, to this relatively inhospitable, infertile outcrop in AD 563?

One possibility is that he knew of it by reputation, and was keen to make his mark on a fledgling Christian community that had already established itself there.

This community was known as the Culdees, who were druids who had converted to Christianity prior to Columba's arrival. Indeed, Iona had previously been known as an important druidical centre, its ancient Gaelic name being Innis nan Druidhnean (lit. island of the druids).

But what drew them to Iona?

Perhaps it was the earth energy that many claim derives from the ancient rock strata on which the island stands. Did it exude a sacred energy that the early Christians, still so intrinsically linked to the mystical druids, could feel and use to enhance their spiritual practices?

Perhaps Iona was influenced by the proximity of Staffa, built of ancient basalt rock, and said by many to tangibly exude earth energy?

Another intriguing possibility is that Columba sought out this island specifically because it was credited with having been visited by Jesus. This is not a particularly unusual story; many ancient sites lay claim to visits by the Son of God, but what gives this one a little sparkle of rarity is that a nearby island is called Eilean Isa, which is Gaelic for the Island of Jesus.

the electric brae

The Electric Brae is to be found on the A719 between Dunure and Croy Bay in Ayrshire. It is a very intriguing physical phenomenon in that, if you put the car brakes on whilst travelling uphill, your vehicle will nonetheless continue to roll slowly upwards.

For years, people believed this was caused by an ancient earth energy, an electromagnetic field contained within the hillside.

However, this attractive idea has been disproved. The Electric Brae is in fact an optical illusion, created by the configuration of the land on either side of the road, which makes what is in fact a downward slope appear to be heading uphill.

sCHiehaLLioN

The word Schiehallion is believed to mean either "The Fairy Mountain of the Caledonians" or the "Holy Hill". Gazing up at it from the best vantage point, the north shore of Loch Rannoch, it is certainly an impressive site, seeming to rise and rise from a quite bleak landscape to form a long ridge ending in a sharp peak.

The physical appearance of a geographical feature should never be underestimated, as this is often key to its mystical significance. Think of a mountain like Uluru, formerly known as Ayers Rock, in the Australian outback. Just looking at it gives you a sense of how powerful and magical, how awe-inspiring it must have seemed to the ancient peoples who lived around it. As cases of fake holy relics – where objects later discovered to have no relation to saints or Christ nonetheless have miraculous events attributed to them – sometimes prove, the power of an object may be all in the human mind. Not that that need be a drawback; the human mind is a hugely powerful instrument.

Not only is Schiehallion impressive to look at but, situated as it is almost in the very centre of Scotland, the views from the summit are incredible, stretching on a clear day as far south as Edinburgh and far north as the Highlands.

Schiehallion is said to house a magic cave, from which those who enter have never returned. Not even, alas, to pinpoint its location on an Ordnance Survey map. The mountain also plays host to a magic well, situated on its Eastern foothills, where local girls gather on the first day of May to dance and drink for good health and fortune in the coming year.

Because it is at the centre of Scotland, and in the path of its major ley lines, this mountain has long been associated with earth energies. Interestingly, it was the location of the first ever measurement of the mass of the earth, conducted by the then Astronomer Royal Nevil Maskelyne. Schiehallion's great mass, enhanced by its uniquely conical shape, caused the pendulum used by this pioneering scientist to swing away from the vertical.

maeshowe, orkney

The low grassy mounds that house the chambered burial cairns at Maeshowe, on Orkney, were built by the islands' neolithic inhabitants untold centuries ago. If, as archeologists suspect, they are of ages with the West coast settlement of Skara Brae, then these cairns may date back as far as 3000 BC.

Visitor numbers are high throughout the year, but the winter solstice on December 22 is said to be the best time to see Maeshowe. This is because the passage running through the main chamber faces South West – that is, directly towards the setting sun at midwinter. Understandably, many believe it was constructed thus deliberately, and that this site was instrinsic to ancient sacred rites centred around what the Celts called the "death of the sun" on the shortest day of the year.

As with many Celtic burial sites, Maeshowe was likely to have been more than simply a repository for the dead. Celtic life, after all, was very much bound up with Celtic death.

For a long period, these cairns were feared because people thought they were the dwellings of fairy folk. They therefore left them undisturbed. Perhaps this was a clever little cooked-up legend, designed to worry strangers and keep them away from this sacred site.

The cairns may also have served the purpose of earmarking land for certain tribes, as noone would take over territory that they could clearly see was guarded by the spirits of the dead.

dowsing and divining

Detecting the presence of earth energies is called divining, or dowsing. There is as yet no technology that can measure earth energies, so dowsers rely on their own human senses, including intuition, and a forked stick in the case of divining for water.

As previously mentioned, areas where earth energies are strong emit telluric energy which, say dowsers, give those who stand there any length of time a sensation akin to hyperactivity; a physical buzzing through the nervous system which can be highly energising or deeply disturbing, depending on whether the energy feels positive or negative.

Alongside points where earth energies are strong are often to be found deep water sources. During the 1930s, a water diviner called Reginald Allender Smith discovered that many ancient sites, such as stone circles, coincided with primary (deep) water sources. This proved to be a major breakthrough for the study of earth energies as it suggested that our ancient ancestors had an intrinsic knowledge of the earth, which they came about without the aid of sophisticated instruments.

If discovering earth energy points gives a diviner a buzzing, enlivening sensation, then discovering primary water sources triggers a quite different, calming sensation. Added to this is a slight tension in the muscles, which is what causes the forked stick, the divining rod, to quiver.

Water diviners have worked in commerical fields for decades, assisting in the discovery of wells and oil sources, which suggests they must be doing something right.

We know that ancient sites often have powerful electromagnetic fields, and that these affect human health and even behaviour, so it seems no great leap to believe that earth energies can be detected through human agency alone.

Ley Lines and ufos

During the 1960s, the first connection was made between UFO sightings and the location of major ley lines. In 1936, Dion Fortune, in her book *The Goat-Foot God*, had suggested that ley lines exuded an energy that not only affected people on earth but also reached out into the wider universe.

In the ensuing decades, others went on to develop this idea of a cosmic force that attracted UFOs, perhaps even helped them navigate across the surface of the Earth, and many UFO sightings have been recorded in areas associated with ley lines.

In 1969, John Mitchell, in The View Over Atlantis, posited a possible connection between cosmic harmonies, mathematical principles and earth energies, arguing that ancient man understood the need to balance his endeavour with the forces of nature. This system is known as geomancy, or the "science of wind and water", and is not dissimilar in principle to the Chinese system of Feng Shui, which seeks to create and channel positive energy through balance and harmony.

Mitchell believed that these forces were at work in the construction of such sacred sites as Stonehenge and the Pyramids – structures which, in their complexity and sheer scale, continue to baffle modern engineers. And which, according to modern ley hunters, are built on important ley line intersections and which some have even suggested operate as portals to other dimensions.

Paul Devereux, a ley line investigator writing in the 1990s, was one such. He believed that sacred sites were erected in order to intensify energy at key points, to create "gateways through which contact with spirits could be achieved". (*Places of Power*, 1990)

To ancient man, the world of spirit may have had similarities with modern-day concepts of extra-terrestrial life; many people believe that extra-terrestrial or alien life forms monitor our activities just as our ancestors once believed the gods did.

There is also a school of thought that aliens offer us salvation, if only we had the sense to understand their message. Others believe they pose a threat, and have predatory designs both on the human race and on the planet itself.

Scottish sightings and the Falkirk Triangle

Scotland is particularly rich in stories of UFO sightings. To the extent that a survey, published in 2002, found that four times as many UFOs were spotted over Scotland every year as France or Italy, the second and third most popular locations respectively.

Caledonian sightings include a giant orb seen hovering, early one morning, over the placid waters of Loch Linnhe in the 1980s and bright orange lights darting across the skies above Cumbernauld during the 1970s.

One area that regularly clocks up more sightings than anywhere else is Bonnybridge, near Falkirk, in central Scotland. It has become so renowned amongst UFOlogists – that is, those who study UFOs – that it is now internationally referred to as the "Falkirk Triangle".

Disappointingly for ley lines enthusiasts however, is the fact that Bonnybridge is not one of the places singled out as a major ley line intersection.

The Bonnybridge phenomena began back in 1979, when a forestry worker called Bob Taylor claimed to have encountered three spherical, hovering objects in the middle of the woods.

It happened on the night of 9th November, when Taylor, walking through forest just off the M8 motorway, emerged into a clearing where he beheld a giant sphere, about 20 feet across, made of a dark metallic material.

As he looked on, two smaller, spiked spheres dropped from the main one and rolled towards him. Attaching themselves to his trouser legs, they drew him towards the main sphere, where he was assaulted by an acrid stench that made him choke and finally lose consciousness. When he awoke, he found himself alone and unable to speak. He staggered home, where his wife called the police.

Though his tale was incredible, they investigated because he a man of previously reliable character, and found strange marks, like ladders, on the ground where Taylor said he had seen the spheres. Ultimately however the trail went cold, though the case remains open.

One theory is that something startled Taylor, prompting an epileptic fit. However, he had never experienced epilepsy either before or since.

Was this then a close encounter of the third kind? Taylor will not be drawn either way, but many UFOlogists believe it is the only explanation and it remains one of the most puzzling cases in the annals of Scottish UFO studies.

Another Bonnybridge name associated with UFO sightings is Craig Malcolm, who has collated video footage of weird sightings over a six year period.

This filmic record includes footage of light balls bouncing along the skyline and a wingless jet which sent a "a black reek belching out the back of it as it soared off."

Malcolm's story begins in 1991, when his brother appeared at his door, ashen and breathless, saying he had been chased by "something". Initially sceptical, the two brothers went out and saw what Craig can only describe as "a figure of eight rotating through the sky. There was no sound; just pulsating lights coming off it. We videoed it and when we played it back, we noticed smaller objects coming off it and flying off in opposite directions."

Since then, he has witnessed 180 unexplained phenomena and amassed 13 hours of footage, which he dispatched to the Search for Extra-terrestrial Intelligence Institute in America for analysis.

"It came back that 95 per cent was UFOs and 5 per cent was aircraft."

Some say that Malcolm's undeniably eerie footage is due to Bonnybridge's close proximity with a gas-flaring terminal and three airports.

He believes there is an earth-bound explanation too; that the lights and objects that litter the sky may be linked to covert military activity.

One time, for example, he and his father were "chased" by two balls of light that came at them on the road home one night. They dashed into their car and drove off, stopping only to ask two men in a red BMW, parked in a nearby lay-by, if they had seen anything.

They had not and "they didn't want to talk to us. The next day the police came to my work - I'd been in a company vehicle the night before - and asked why I'd been on that road. By the end of the week, I'd lost my job."

Malcolm adds that he knows it is a cliché to "blame the government" - "but I worked for the Ministry of Defence ... and had my eyes opened. I drove senior staff to and from military establishments all over the place – there's a lot more out there than people believe."

Not everyone is convinced by Malcolm's ideas. Some insist that the mysterious lights and objects associated with UFO sightings are caused either by natural phenomena, such as ball lightning or sun spots, or flying debris from broken up satellites.

Nevertheless, there are over 300 reported UFO sightings a year in Bonnybridge, though what draws them here, to this quite unremarkable town which has neither wide open spaces nor ancient sites to recommend it, remains a puzzle.

Even the UFOlogists are stumped. Ron Halliday, who has written two books on UFOs, believes Bonnybridge may serve as a portal to another dimension but has, as yet, no proof to back this idea up.

Meantime, visitors from across Europe and even the USA flock to this area of Scotland, hoping to experience something of its other-worldly magic.

supernatural creatures

Scotland was and is a nation of storytellers and wild geographical features, from sudden mountains to untamed wilderness to hidden lochins and secret caves.

Given these factors, it is perhaps little wonder that Scotland is also home to a huge array of supernatural creatures, from the monster who haunts the depths of Loch Ness to the wailing banshee-like women who stalk the lone traveller.

It is highly unlikely that these creatures existed, though there are theories as to how the legends came about. Selkies, for example, were believed to be seals who could take on the form of a man. But many now speculate that it is seals' natural, almost human expressions that gave rise to this myth. It also served as a way of explaining the terrible toll that the sea exacted on coastal communities dependent on fishing.

Furthermore, there was surely something comforting in the notion that seals and mermaids had a human connection and were capable of forming relationships with ordinary men and women as it meant they would protect us on the high seas, guiding us safely into harbour.

Similarly, the legends pertaining to giants were probably created as a means of understanding why the landscape, with its sharp mountains and scatterings of boulders, came about. Geology was centuries hence and so the idea of a long gone race of giants flinging rocks about as they fought with each other was a means of making sense of the inexplicable.

Add to that that a society always needs heroies, preferably legendary ones capable of mighty feats, and you can see why Scotland, like so many nations, loves its giants and man-eating monsters.

These stories were passed down through the generations by word of mouth, and were informed by stories brought by contact, through war, trade and migration, with other nations, such as Norway and Ireland.

The tales of the Fians, a mythical race of Irish heroes, crossed the Irish Sea and found a second home in Scotland while the selkie, the kelpie and the mermaid, a stock feature of our national tales, are shared between Scotland, Ireland and Scandanavia and have provided material for some of our favourite ballads as well as stories.

The oral tradition was dominant in Gaelic-speaking communities right up until the 19th century and, as these things go, it is inevitable that the tales became ever more fanciful in the telling.

Many relate to the sea, that ocean of uncertainty of which people lived in fear and to which countless superstitions attach themselves.

Others serve to explain the landscape or warn people of the ways of the fairy-folk.

And many relate to death, featuring eerie figures who warn of imminent doom or presage fearful events.

tales of the sea

Throughout history, many of the people of Scotland have made their living from the sea. The waters around the coast of Scotland can be treacherous and the weather harsh and unpredictable, and none are more aware of the dangers that they face than those who sail these waters. Given the many hazards of their occupation, it is not surprising that Scottish fisherfolk and sailors have always been superstitious. It is a trait that they share with seafaring people all over the world. The legends about the mysteries that lie beneath the seas around the globe have many features in common, and it is not only in Scotland that tales of man's encounters with creatures of the deep are told. There are two broad categories of creature that feature in these stories. The first category includes a variety of harmful creatures, some monstrous, that put the lives of seafarers in peril by causing storms, sinking ships, blowing vessels off course, and so on. The second category, to which mermaids and seal people belong, are creatures which have been said not only to interact with human beings, but from time to time, to have interbred with them.

Sea monsters feature in legends the world over. They are blamed for missing ships, unexpected storms and mysterious drownings. Some can emerge from their watery lair and cause devastation on land.

Many people will think of the mermaid as a fabulous creature formed by the imagination of Hans Anderson, whose story of the Little Mermaid is widely known. But in times gone by, mermaids were believed to be real. With a human head and torso and a fish tail, mer-people, and in particular mermaids, were allegedly sighted at various coastal sites around Scotland on numerous occasions over many years. In Scandinavia, belief in mermaids took hold a very long time ago, and in Scotland too, stories of the mer-folk date back over centuries. Many a fisherman has allegedly fallen for the charms of one of these fabulous creatures and few of their stories have happy endings.

The seal-folk, silkies or selkies as they are known in Scotland, resemble ordinary seals while in the water and change into human form when they come ashore and shed their skins. It was widely believed, not only in Scotland but also in Ireland and Scandinavia that seals were in fact humans, who had been put under a spell. Most of the time, it was said, these people were condemned to live as seals, but from time to time they could change back into human form. In Scotland and in Ireland, the seal people were believed to have the power of changing into human form when they came onto land and shed their skins. If their skins were stolen from them, they could not return to the sea but had to live as humans. Many children were allegedly born out of unions between humans and seal folk, and the people of the Clan MacCodrum of the Outer Hebrides were said to have been descended from a seal-woman who married an islander. The Shetland and Orkney Isles are a particularly rich source of selkie legends. The story of the crofter and the seal-woman is of uncertain origin and has a number of slightly different versions. One version of the story comes from Shetland, another from Orkney. Other versions place the story on the Scottish mainland, or on other islands. As so often happens with tales of this sort, it has also blended with mermaid legend and very similar stories are told of a fisherman and a mermaid. Wherever the tale was first told, and whether it was first the story of mermaids or a seal folk, it has found a place in the imaginations of all those who have ever believed in these fabulous creatures.

The crofter and the seal-woman

There was once a young crofter who had a patch of land by the sea, where he eked out a meagre living, growing a few basic food crops. He had a small boat and used this to supplement his income, setting crab and lobster pots on the seabed along the shoreline when the weather permitted, and selling his catch locally.

One evening, as the crofter was walking by the shore towards the cove where he kept his boat tied up on the beach, he heard the sound of women's laughter coming from behind a rocky outcrop close to the water's edge. The crofter moved closer, his instincts telling him he should not make a sound that might disturb the revellers. He peered over the top of the rocks and saw a group of beautiful women with long, silken hair, dancing on a small stretch of sand at the water's edge. The crofter suspected at once that these must be seal-women, and, sure enough, his suspicions were confirmed when he saw that laid out on the rocks behind the dancing figures, were the magical skins which they had shed when they came ashore.

The sun began to go down, but the women danced on, unaware of their silent watcher. The crofter was transfixed. There was one among them who had caught his eye, and he could not take his gaze from her. Her eyes were as black as night and her hair fell about her shoulders in a shimmering curtain of gold. Her skin glowed, an opalescent white tinged with pink by the rosy light of sunset. She was the most beautiful thing he had ever seen.

The tide was coming in and bit by bit, the water was creeping further up the sand. The seal-women stopped dancing and moved towards the rocks, ready to gather up their skins and return to the sea. Last to come was the one who had stolen the heart of the crofter. One by one, the beautiful creatures grasped their skins and slipped them onto their bodies, pulling the silver-grey cowls over their heads. But just as the last one was reaching out for hers, the crofter jumped from his hiding place and took a hold of it. He could not bear to see her change back into a seal and disappear. When the seal-woman's companions saw what had happened, they knew they could do nothing to help her. With a cry of despair, they slipped back into the sea and disappeared. A few moments later, the head of a bull seal broke the surface. The poor creature stared helplessly towards shore, with anguish in its eyes. It was the husband of the seal-woman.

The seal-woman begged the crofter to give her back her skin, and let her return to her home and her family, but the crofter's passion made him selfish. He could not bring himself to do as she wished. He asked her to become his wife. He swore that he would make her happy in a new life with him on land and that he would care for her as long as he lived. The seal-woman was trapped. She had no choice but to agree, and so the crofter led her back to his cottage. He tried to soothe her with kind words and promises, but still he could not set her free, and clutched the sealskin tight against his chest to keep it safe from her. He waited until late at night when she had finally fallen asleep, then he took the skin and wrapped it carefully in blankets. He placed the bundle in a wooden box, and hid it in beneath some straw in the darkest corner of the byre, where he knew she would never find it.

Years passed. The crofter was blissfully happy with his beautiful wife. They had seven healthy children and life was good. The crofter worked hard to support his family, and although they were not rich, they had everything they needed. The seal-woman was a good wife and mother, and turned the crofter's house into a warm and loving home. The crofter loved her more than he could ever say, and she, for her part, was very fond of him, but in spite of all her husband's kindness and the great love she had for her children, she could never forget the place she had come from. She had once been completely happy, and nothing that the crofter could say or do would ever compensate her for her loss. Sometimes, late at night, when the family was asleep, she slipped away from the cottage and tiptoed to the water's edge. She would stand there for most of the night, staring out to sea, remembering her lost kinfolk and hoping for a glimpse of their heads bobbing up and down in the moonlit waters. Somewhere out there, waiting for her, was her first husband, a selkie just like she, and her heart was still with him.

One day, when the crofter was out working in the fields, the seal-woman was in the cottage preparing food when the youngest child came running in, carrying something in his arms. He had found the wooden box that had been hidden so long ago in the corner of the byre. With a child's natural curiosity, he had opened it and discovered the sealskin concealed inside. The boy knew nothing about his mother's past. He only wanted to ask her what it was he had found, that felt so soft and warm, and had the fresh, salty smell of the sea in its silvery hairs. The seal-woman gently took it from him, her eyes filling with tears.

When the crofter came home that night, the cottage was strangely quiet. The children were all fast asleep in their beds, and a pot of soup bubbled gently on the fire, but his wife was not there to greet him, and there was nothing to indicate where she might have gone. A sudden fear gripped the crofter's heart and he ran out to the byre. When he found the wooden box open and its contents gone, he thought his heart would break. The seal-woman had gone back to her own folk, and to the husband she had before him.

In time the crofter found another wife, a good, kind woman who loved him dearly and cared for his children as if they were her own. He was content with his lot. But sometimes, late at night, just as the seal-woman had done before him, he would slip away on his own and stand at the water's edge, staring out to sea, straining his eyes for one last glimpse of his first and only true love.

The mermaid's revenge

There are almost as many Scottish stories told about merfolk as there are about selkies, for people were equally fascinated with these creatures that were half human and half fish. Mermen and mermaids were believed to be able to shed their fish tails when they came onto dry land, just as selkies could shed their skins.

But while the stories of the selkie people almost exclusively conjure up an image of a gentle creature which could be surprisingly forgiving to man in spite of his cruelty, some of the tales of the mer-people show mermaids in a less kindly light. A mermaid could make a man fall in love with her, but she could also lure him to his death. And woe betide the human who crossed a mermaid, as the following story illustrates.

There was once a merchant who lived by the sea, in a grand house overlooking a sandy cove. At the edge of the cove there was a large, black rock. This rock had been worn so smooth by the waves that its surface gleamed, and the top of it was so comfortably rounded that it looked just like a plump, well-feathered cushion. It was the favourite seat of a mermaid. Every night she came to the cove and sat upon the rock, stretching out her tail over the polished stone so that it shimmered in the moonlight. Then she began to sing. The merchant and his wife were sound sleepers and although they heard the eerie sound of the mermaid's singing from time to time, it did not disturb them unduly. They were used to it. But when the merchant's wife gave birth to her first child, everything changed.

The baby seemed contented enough during the day, but every night, after darkness had fallen, he would grow fretful and begin to cry. Once he started, nothing would console him, and the nursemaid who cared for him became exhausted with the effort of trying to soothe his tears. The baby's crying disturbed his mother as well, preventing her from sleeping. She took turns with the nursemaid, walking up and down the nursery floor with her son in her arms as she tried in vain to rock him to sleep. One night as she was doing this, the child paused in his crying to draw breath for a few seconds. There was silence in the nursery, but outside, the merchant's wife could hear the sound of the mermaid singing in the darkness, and she realised that it was the singing that was upsetting her son. It was only at night that the child cried, and it was only at night that the mermaid sang.

The next night, a servant from the house was sent to speak to the mermaid, to ask her to stop her singing, or to move away. The request was politely made, but rudely refused. There was a note of defiance in the songs that the mermaid sang that night, and the sound could be clearly heard in every room of the merchant's house. And so it went on. Several times, the mermaid was begged to stop her singing, but every time she was approached, her response was to sing all the louder. And the louder she sang, the louder the baby cried.

The merchant's wife reached the end of her tether. She called her male servants together and told them to go down to the shore with hammers and pickaxes, to smash the mermaid's rock to pieces. The men did as she had asked, and by the end of the day, there was nothing left of the rock but a heap of small, black, jagged stones. Now, perhaps, the mermaid would accept defeat gracefully and find another place to sing her strange songs.

But when the mermaid reached shore that evening and saw what had been done, not a thought of defeat crossed her mind. She was beside herself with rage that her beautiful singing stone had been destroyed, and she was determined to get her revenge. She lifted her voice to a pitch that it had never reached before, and screamed out a curse that was carried by the wind coming in from the sea, right to the ears of the merchant's wife. The mermaid's words struck horror into the hearts of all those who heard them. The venom and strength in her tone were terrible to hear, as she shrieked that tragedy would descend upon the household, and that the merchant's family line would die out. Upstairs in the nursery, the force of the sound began to rock the baby's cradle back and forth, back and forth, with increasing violence. When mermaid's last, terrible song was over, the merchant's wife hurried upstairs to attend to her child. She found him lying dead beneath his upturned cradle. Just as the mermaid had predicted, there were no more children, and the merchant died without an heir to succeed him.

The Blue Men

Selkies and mermaids were said to dwell in many places around the coast of Scotland, but the Blue Men are a phenomenon to be found in only one place. Between the Island of Lewis and the Shiant Isles lies a narrow strait, part of the Minch, which is known in Gaelic as *Sruth nam Fear Gorm* – The Stream of the Blue Men. Even when the seas all around are calm, the water in the Stream of the Blue Men can be rough and treacherous, and even today many skippers choose to steer clear of the strait and take a more circuitous route, for fear of the Blue Men. Anyone who has been at sea when the weather is wild, or has seen the force with which white-capped waves, several feet high, come crashing in to shore when a storm is blowing, can imagine how it is possible that sailors, caught in the teeth of a storm, might conjure up in their minds a picture of raging, white-haired blue figures attacking their boat. But if the Blue Men are no more than mental images which spring to into the heads of seamen in storm-tossed ships, then why are there no Blue Men anywhere else in the waters around Scotland, or even around the world?

The Blue Men were said to live in underwater caves in the Minch, and to occupy themselves by churning up the waters in the strait by the Shiant Isles. Sometimes they slept, and it was only then that the waters in the strait settled down to peace for a brief spell. As soon as the Blue Men awoke, the waves would rise. The Blue Men would stir the waters with their long arms, scattering spray and foam all around. They took particular pleasure in attacking boats. They posted sentinels at the entrance to the strait and when a boat approached, the sentinels would signal to their companions lying in wait under the water, who would then come to the surface to stir up trouble. They would thrust their heads and chests out of the water and frighten the watching sailors. They would hurl abuse at the skipper, and jostle and shove the vessels to make them turn over, or pull on the rudder to force a ship off course and onto the rocks. Some folk referred to the strait as The Current of Destruction, and with good reason. Several boats were wrecked in the waters of the strait, and many times the blame for the disaster was placed upon the malicious activities of the Blue Men.

It was said that one way to outwit the Blue Men was to develop a skill in composing rhyming couplets, and the following tale illustrates this belief.

The Blue Men were lying dozing beneath the waves when the sentinels gave warning that a large ship was approaching. They swam to the surface in their hordes. They could see the great white sails of the vessel in the distance. It was a big ship, and they would have their work cut out for them if they were to capsize this one. The ship moved into the strait and several of the Blue Men dived below the surface and pulled on the keel, but the vessel moved on, sure and steady, and their efforts were to no avail. Others swarmed along the sides of the ship, thumping it with their fists, but the ship was built of the strongest, thickest timbers and they could not punch a hole in it. Nor could they move the rudder. The ship stayed right on course, steering a safe path through the strait. The chief of the Blue Men rose up out of the waves in fury. As he had done so often before with other ships, he challenged the skipper to a battle in verse.

'Man of the black cap, what do you say
As your proud ship cleaves the brine?'
The skipper did not hesitate to reply.
'My speedy ship takes the shortest way
And I'll follow you line by line.'
The chief of the Blue Men continued the challenge.
'My men are eager, my men are ready
To drag you beneath the waves!'
But the skipper was undaunted. His response came
back, quick as a flash.
'My ship is speedy, my ship is steady;
If it sank it would wreck your caves.'

The chief of the Blue Men knew he had been beaten. No skipper had ever been able to answer his challenges so quickly and so cleverly. He could have no power over such a skipper, or his ship. Reluctantly, he signalled to his men and they sank below the waves. The ship sailed on through the strait unharmed, its tall mast straight and true and its snow-white sails puffed out with pride.

MONSTERS

Nessie

The most famous monster in Scotland is the beast that is said to live in the deep dark waters of Loch Ness. Affectionately known as Nessie, the monster is generally referred to as 'she', although there has never been an opportunity for anyone to determine the sex of this mythical creature. Nessie attracts visitors from all over the world, tourists, reporters and scientific investigators, and over the years has been subjected to more camera surveillance than any 'reality TV' programme participant is ever likely to have to endure. In spite of this, she remains elusive, guarding her privacy carefully in the hidden murky depths of the loch, rewarding the thousands of hopeful spectators who come to see her with no more than the occasional tantalising glimpse of what she might, or might not, look like.

The first written record of a beast in Loch Ness is in Saint Adamnan's biography of Saint Columba, which was written in the seventh century AD. According to Adamnan, Saint Columba was walking along the shore of the loch in 565AD when he caught sight of an enormous creature in the water, ready to attack a man who was swimming there. Saint Columba ordered the beast to depart in the name of God, and it obeyed him. On another occasion Saint Columba encountered the creature again, lying in wait for a victim. Saint Columba commanded the monster never to harm a human being again, and since then, there have been no reports of the Loch Ness monster having threatened anyone.

Over the years, the Loch Ness monster seems to have surfaced from time to time, giving rise to a number of stories about the beast in the loch, but it was only in the twentieth century that Nessie's name came to real prominence. In the 1930s, a road was built alongside the northern shore of the loch. This brought a growth in the number of people visiting the area and also afforded passers-by a clear view of the loch from their cars. In 1933, Nessie hit the headlines of the *Inverness Courier*. A couple who lived in the district claimed to have seen an enormous creature thrashing about in the surface waters of the loch. The article in the *Courier* marked the beginning of Nessie's meteoric rise to fame. It was not long before she had allegedly been sighted on land, casually crossing the road by the loch one day in early summer. Loch Ness Monster fever rapidly spread and Nessie became national headlines as groups of people swarmed to the shores of Loch Ness hoping to see, or catch, the creature who dwelt therein. In August of that year, when the fever was at its peak, there were no less than nine alleged sightings of the monster in the water. In July 1934, there were at least eight more. Less than a year later, however, the first wave of monster-hunting began to peter out after some plaster-casts of large animal footprints, which were said to belong to the monster, were exposed as hoaxes. How many of the claimed sightings had been fakes?

In spite of the scepticism of many, interest in the possibility of a mysterious creature dwelling in the loch did not go away entirely. Sightings continued to be reported from time to time in the years that followed, and in the 1960s, monster fever seemed to take a hold of the public imagination once again. With the resurgence in public interest came another increase in the number of alleged sightings. The summer of 1966 was particularly busy. The 1970s and '80s seem to have been a time of general cynicism, or short-sightedness, for scarcely a handful of sightings were recorded, but in the 1990s, armed with the wonders of sophisticated photography, video cameras, etc., members of the public took up the hunt once more.

So, if the Loch Ness monster does exist, or has ever existed, what sort of creature might she be? In the days of Saint Columba, she was seen (or imagined) to be one of the kelpies, or water horses, mythical creatures which were believed to prey on unsuspecting human victims, particularly children, luring them onto their backs before dragging them down into the water, never to be seen again. In more recent times, she has been described as having between one and three humps, which are somewhere between four and forty feet in length and are commonly said to resemble an upturned boat. She has been said to have a long tail and a long neck, around six feet long. Her mouth may be approximately one foot wide. When submerging and moving off, she makes a great splash and leaves a v-shaped wake behind her. Of course although the creature is commonly referred to as *the* Loch Ness monster (singular), it cannot be possible that there has only been one creature surviving nearly fifteen hundred years since the days of Saint Columba. There must have been, at least, a succession of breeding pairs over the centuries, and the fact that on a few occasions not one, but two 'monster wakes' have allegedly been spotted simultaneously, seems to support this theory. The one identifiable creature which Nessie can be said to resemble most closely is the plesiosaur, which was a carnivorous marine reptile of the Jurassic and Cretaceous periods. Plesiosaurs could grow to around forty feet in length, had long necks and turtle-shaped bodies, and had paddle-like flippers to propel themselves through the water. There are many people who believe that Nessie is a plesiosaur, and although the survival of a family of such creatures in one isolated place in Scotland is hard to explain when all the others became extinct sixty-five million years ago, there have been attempts to demonstrate that such a thing is possible. One theory suggests that some plesiosaur eggs, long frozen in some deep, cold recess of the loch, could have thawed out and hatched to start the new dynasty. The cynics continue to contest the theory by stating that the loch does not have an adequate supply of food for such a creature, and so argument is met with counter-argument *ad nauseam*.

Loch Ness is huge, dark, and deep. Much of its waters are literally unfathomable, and this is perhaps the biggest hurdle, both for all those who wish to prove Nessie's existence, and those who wish to disprove it. The mystery is kept at the forefront of the public's imagination with boat trips and sightseeing tours around the loch on offer for visiting tourists, and a Loch Ness Monster Exhibition at the local visitor centre. Alleged sightings are faithfully recorded in detail, and video footage of gloomy, unidentifiable shapes in the water is studied closely by enthusiasts and sceptics alike. For the real Nessie fan, the opportunity to look for the monster on webcam from the comfort of their own home has taken the hunt into the twenty-first century. The legend continues to grow.

Morag of Loch Morar

Loch Morar is not as large in surface area as Loch Ness, but the water there is deeper, and it is said that hundreds of feet below the surface of the loch lives another monster, who has come to be known as Morag. Morag has not reached the same dizzy heights of stardom as Nessie, and her history is not as long, but for those who are fascinated with mythical creatures of the deep, the possibility of her existence is no less exciting.

The earliest recorded sightings of the Loch Morar monster date from the second half of the nineteenth century. From time to time, fishermen out on the loch, or walkers making their way along its rocky shores, would claim to have seen one or more dark humps in the water, like upturned boats. Superstitions about death and dying were still very much a part of life in the Highlands in those days, and some said that these strange sights were omens of death, ghostly boats that warned of some tragedy to come. Others were not so sure, for they were convinced that the humps were a part of something living, some mysterious creature that rarely allowed itself to be seen. Years passed, and the rumours of the creature grew slowly. Eventually, as Nessie had done, this creature acquired a name, but still she remained reclusive, and she is still less sought-after than Nessie.

Many of the people who claimed to have seen Morag were fishing on the loch at the time. The sight of her hump (or humps), appearing and disappearing in the water, have caused great perplexity to a number of people over the years. In the 1960s, Morag was allegedly responsible for ruining an entire day's fishing for two young men. They were rowing out into the loch, and saw what the thought was a smooth, rounded rocky outcrop sticking out of the water, so they started to navigate their way round the obstacle with care. Their boat was hired, and they had no wish to pay for any damages they might incur with a careless bump. They were only half way round this miniature island when it suddenly moved, then sank, bumping into their little boat on the way down and making ripples of such a size that they almost capsized. Forgetting all about fishing, or the price they had paid for a day's boat hire, the two young men rowed back to shore as quickly as possible. There, with wide eyes and white faces, they returned the boat to its puzzled owner, muttering as they did so about the dangers 'out there'.

Descriptions of Morag, who has been seen mostly in the water, but also, on at least one occasion, on shore, make her sound very similar in appearance to her famous friend in Loch Ness. She is dark in colour – brownish-black or black. Her skin is bumpy, like that of a reptile. She has been variously described as having one, two, three or four humps, and it is thought that she is around thirty feet long. Like Nessie, she has a long neck. One man who claimed to have seen her also said that he found her footprints in some soft ground on the shore, and they were diamond-shaped. A monster spotter with artistic leanings, Dr George Cooper, painted her portrait in 1958, but as Morag rarely reveals more of herself than a hump here and a neck there, it is hard to tell whether Dr Cooper managed to capture a true likeness. Those who have the time, energy and enthusiasm to continue the search will maybe be rewarded with the chance to see for themselves one day in the future.

Loch Morar is more remote and less easily accessible than Loch Ness, and most of the time, Morag is left in peace. Every now and then, another alleged sighting is logged in the records of keen cryptozoologists, but most visitors to the area barely give her more than a passing thought, and her presence is not advertised. For those who live close to Loch Morar, it is probably a good thing that Morag has not drawn the same attention to herself as Nessie. There is no monster exhibition, and local people are, for the most part, reluctant to exploit the monster rumours in any way. But monster enthusiasts are a die-hard bunch, and for them the legend lives on, even if it breathes more quietly than the legend of Nessie. And the theories about what she might be are much the same; like Nessie, she is now most commonly believed to be a plesiosaur – it may be possible, some say, that Nessie and Morag are related. It has even been suggested that far, far underground, there is a long water-filled tunnel that connects Loch Ness with Loch Morar and that the Loch Ness Monster and the Loch Morar Monster are one and the same creature, travelling between the two sites. Perhaps she likes to keep the visitors entertained. Or perhaps, in the way that all film stars do, the monster sometimes tires of all the cameras and attention. At times like these, we might imagine that she takes a break from life in Loch Ness and goes to Loch Morar to annoy a few fishermen for a change.

Nessie and Morag are the two most famous loch-dwelling monsters in Scotland, but, if we are to believe in their existence, we must also give some credence to the claims that in several other Scottish lochs – Loch Garten and Loch Oich, for example, similar creatures have been sighted. If all the claims are true, there could be as many as twenty loch monsters, perhaps even more!

The Linton Worm

There are a number of references to 'worms' in traditional Scottish stories. The monster that is said to live in Loch Morar, for example, was once known as 'The Great Worm'. Several sites around the country are said to have been, once upon a time, the dwelling place of a worm. These worms were great serpents, which were said to terrorise the surrounding countryside, killing the farmers' animals and attacking humans. Some were believed to have magical powers. Others had rank, poisonous breath.

The story of the worm of Linton belongs to the Scottish Borders, where long ago, in Roxburghshire, it is said that a fearsome serpent used to live in a hollow on the slopes of Linton Hill near Jedburgh. For years the Linton worm blighted the lives of the people living in the district. Its breath was said to be so poisonous that if a man inhaled the slightest whiff of it, he faced instant death, so no-one dared approach it. Farmers stood by helplessly as their sheep and cattle dwindled in numbers, snapped up, one by one, by the ravenous jaws of the worm. No man had the courage to try to kill it, for it seemed like an impossible task, sure to end in death for anyone who attempted it.

Then a man called John Sommerville of Lauriston heard about the beast, and decided to come and see the worm for himself. Following the directions given to him be some people who lived nearby, Sommerville rode his horse cautiously towards the hollow where the terrible creature lay resting. He stopped his horse at a safe distance from the worm's lair and waited. The wind carried the scent of a human towards the sleeping beast, and slowly it woke up, and reared up its ugly head to find where the scent was coming from. Sommerville kept a tight hold of the horse's reins and remained perfectly still. At the sight of the man and the horse together, the worm seemed perplexed. It stretched out its neck and opened its jaws to their fullest extent, but it did not attack. It gave out a great puff of its fiery venomous breath, but Sommerville was too far away to feel its effects, and the poisonous gas dispersed in the air before it reached him. Still the serpent remained motionless, its jaws gaping helplessly. The sight gave Sommerville much food for thought. It was clear that although a single cow, or sheep, or even a man would make an easy mouthful for the beast, the prospect of man and horse together had it puzzled, for the two were more than its jaws could cope with.

As he turned and rode back home, a cunning plan was forming in Sommerville's mind. The next day, he went to the local blacksmith and asked him to make a special lance. The lance had to be much longer than such a weapon would normally be, for Sommerville had to keep a safe distance from the monster's breath. At the end of the lance was to be a spiked wheel made of the strongest iron.

When the lance had been finished to his satisfaction, Sommerville prepared to do battle. Taking his most loyal servant along with him, he rode into Jedburgh carrying his customised weapon and declared that soon the Linton worm would be dead. Not surprisingly, his claims were met with jeers and derision, for what he claimed, according to the people of Jedburgh, was impossible. Nonetheless, a number of townsfolk followed him out to Linton Hill, and selecting a viewpoint as close to the worm's hollow as they dared go, settled down to watch the action.

Sommerville rode closer to the worm's lair. His servant followed on foot. Sommerville reined in his horse and the servant took a ball of peat dipped in pitch from the bag he carried on his back, and stuck it firmly onto the spiked wheel at the end of Sommerville's lance. They moved a little closer. Just as before, the serpent caught the scent of human flesh and reared up its head. Just as it had done before, it stretched out its neck and opened its jaws to their fullest extent. At a signal from his master, the servant set fire to the peat ball on Sommerville's lance, and set it spinning. Sommerville spurred his horse into a gallop, charged up to the open-mouthed worm, and thrust his lance as far as he could down its throat. The serpent writhed in fury and pain as the fiery peat ball seared his gullet and the spikes pierced his flesh, but it had been mortally wounded, and after one or two moments of desperate struggling, it stopped moving and died.

Sir John Sommerville had become a hero, and as reward for his courage, he was knighted, becoming the first Baron of Linton. At

Linton Kirk nearby, a stone was carved to commemorate the great occasion when the people of Linton were saved from the worm. And on the landscape of Linton Hill, the strange undulating marks caused by the worm as it writhed and struggled before death still remain.

The Big Grey Man of Ben Macdhui

Ben Macdhui is the highest peak in the Cairngorms, and the second highest in Scotland. From its summit, the climber is afforded a magnificent panorama of the surrounding peaks; Cairngorm, Ben Avon and Cairn Toul. To the north west, the River Spey passes through Aviemore on its way to the Moray Firth. To the east, the Dee flows towards Ballater, Aboyne and Aberdeen. The mountain is popular with climbers who visit the region from many different countries, and its slopes offer a number of routes that are both challenging and rewarding, even to experienced mountaineers. But Ben Macdhui is well-known not only for its beauty and the sport that it offers its visitors. For over a century now, there has been much speculation that there may be something frightening lurking on Ben Macdhui. Over this period, several climbers claim to have witnessed a mysterious presence on the mountain; many believe it to be a physical one. This presence has been named *Am Fear Liath Mor*, more commonly known as The Big Grey Man.

On remote mountain slopes, far from the noise and bustle of centres of population, it is easy to give full reign to the imagination and let the mind wander to strange apparitions and monsters. There are plenty of things that the mountain climber encounters to provide fuel for the mind's journey; strange echoes in gullies, tricks of the light, shapes in the mist, ominous shadows cast as the sun moves across the unfamiliar landscape. Human beings are social animals, and solitude is alien to most of us. It can alter one's perceptions, especially in an unfamiliar environment, and fear of real, physical and recognisable danger can find itself accompanied by a fear of unidentifiable, intangible threats, which come from a realm far removed from man's knowledge of the physical world and its nature.

It is easier to dismiss the legends of monstrous apparitions in the mountains around the world than it is to give credence to them. The existence of the creatures in these legends has never been proved beyond doubt by material evidence or scientific fact. The Yeti in the Himlayas, Bigfoot in North America, and the Spectre of the Brocken in Germany are all similar in this respect; they are beasts seen, but not captured, perceived but not touched. Some believe that there is a physical presence of some kind where these creatures have allegedly been seen. Most people, on the other hand, do not, and react to the legends with scepticism or derision. The Yeti and Bigfoot feature in cartoons from time to time, as cuddly figures of fun. The Spectre of the Brocken in dismissed in more scientific fashion, as a shadowy illusion created by sunlight and mist.

The Big Grey Man of Ben Macdhui, like the other monstrous apparitions, has allegedly been seen and heard on a number of different occasions. But there is another more sinister aspect to the Grey Man, which the other apparitions do not share. The Big Grey Man's presence is not perceived by the physical senses alone. It can make itself felt in the spirits, in a manner that is generally claimed to be very disturbing. It is alleged that the Grey Man exerts a strong psychic influence upon those who encounter him. And several climbers, after having undergone the experience, have been reluctant to return to the mountain.

The first time the possible existence of the Big Grey Man of Ben Macdhui was mentioned in Scotland was in 1925. Norman Collie, a professor in Chemistry from London and an experienced and well-respected mountaineer, related his story to members of the Cairngorm Club at their Annual General Meeting. He recalled a solo climb on the mountain in 1891, and said that as he was making his way back down the mountainside from the summit through the mist, he became aware of the sound of footsteps behind him. For every three or four steps that the professor took, he heard one of these footsteps, as if whoever – or whatever – was following him taking much larger strides than himself. At first, he dismissed the sounds as nonsense, for he could see nothing, but as he continued downwards he could still hear them. At this point he was overwhelmed by a feeling of terror, and in blind panic, took flight, descending the rest of the mountain with more concern for speed than safety on the treacherous terrain. The experience had left him badly shaken, and determined that he would never climb Ben Macdhui alone again, for there was something 'very queer' about the higher slopes of the mountain.

Collie had told this story once before, some years earlier in New Zealand, and it had been greeted with a moderate degree of interest and some understandable scepticism. But when Dr A M Kellas had heard about it, he was more than moderately interested in Collie's experience. Dr Kellas was another well-known figure in mountaineering circles, much respected for his achievements climbing in the Himalayas, who later died during the first expedition to Mount Everest in 1921–22. When Kellas heard Collie's story, he wrote to him to tell him of his own experience. Kellas had been on Ben Macdhui with his brother, and had been hammering out crystals from some rocks quite close to the summit when they had become aware of a large figure descending from above, out of the mist. The two men had then, like Collie, succumbed to a terrible feeling of fear and had been compelled to flee.

We do not know why Collie waited 34 years to tell his story to the Cairngorm Club, but it is reasonable to assume that he might have felt apprehensive about the reception it might get. Perhaps the letter from Kellas helped to give Collie the courage to relate his account of the experience. But at any rate, when he did finally speak out in 1925, he would know that there was at least one other knowledgeable, reasonable and experienced man who had testified to having had a similar encounter. Both men had spent extended amounts of time in remote mountain regions and consequently knew all too well the tricks that could be played on the mind when a person was alone, cold and tired. They were also familiar with the strange sights and sounds of such places; shadows in the mist, falling rocks, echoes and suchlike. But both strenuously denied that the phenomenon they had witnessed was anything like this.

There have been several reports of alleged encounters with the Big Grey Man since then. Some of them, undoubtedly, have been fantasy, or hoax. Others cannot be dismissed so easily. Some people claim to have heard strange voices, speaking in a foreign tongue, which has been said to resemble either Gaelic, or Urdu. Others have said that they could hear hauntingly beautiful music. Alleged sightings vary from a vague description of a hazy, large, upright figure to a more precise picture of something akin to the Sasquatch or Yeti. In 1944, Captain Sir Hugh Rankin claimed to have met and spoken with the Big Grey Man on two separate occasions. According to Sir Hugh, who was a Buddhist himself, the Grey Man was a Bodhisattwa. [A Bodhisattwa is a being in an advanced degree of incarnation, next to that of a Buddha, who has achieved enlightenment and acts as a guide to others in their progress towards the same.] Sir Hugh was humbled, but unafraid. His experience of the Big Grey Man was apparently wholly benign. But most other climbers who have tales to tell of the Big Grey Man or of out-of-the-ordinary experiences on Ben Macdhui have shared feelings that are much different from those felt by Sir Hugh Rankin. Fear, sudden and overwhelming, has been commonly reported and openly admitted, even by hardened men of the outdoors. Sudden, terrible feelings of depression have also been described on a number of occasions. In some men's experience, these feelings have rapidly led to thoughts of suicide and frightening compulsions to self harm by falling or jumping off a ledge or into a gully. This power that the phenomenon of the Grey Man seems to exert over people's minds is what makes it uniquely sinister and dangerous. Perhaps, knowing something about the phenomenon, the fear of an encounter with the Big Grey Man that has both triggered and inflamed the imaginations of many climbers on the slopes of Ben Macdhui, affecting their mood and convincing them that such an encounter has taken place. But that does not explain why Collie and Kellas felt as they did, on separate occasions and quite independently of each other. Nor will all climbers since then have known about the phenomenon before they set off up the mountain.

The phenomenon may be nothing more than a collection of misperceptions, or optical and aural illusions. It may be hallucination induced by fatigue, or hysteria. Norman Collie may have had a panic attack. Dr Kellas may have seen his own shadow in the mist. But their refusal to dismiss their experience as illusion or panic persisted until their deaths. Furthermore, there are several people still alive who claim to have experienced the Big Grey Man – whatever it is. And like Collie and Kellas, those among them whose claims were made in good faith are unlikely ever to be convinced that there is not 'something up there.'

the fairy realm

Belief in fairies was prevalent in Scotland in days gone by. Although they were spiritual beings, fairies were thought to resemble human beings in many ways; their physical appearance was similar, they lived together in social communities, they ate, drank, danced and sang, they could be kind, or malicious, charitable or unforgiving. Fairies were invisible to the human eye for most of the time, but when they did allow themselves to be seen, they were most commonly described as slender and pale, with gold-red hair, dressed in green. Most of them were, or appeared as women.

Opinions differed as to what, or who, the fairies were. Some people believed they were fallen angels, or demons. Others thought that they were the spirits of the dead. Other people simply saw them as another class of being, inhabitants of a world that existed separately from the human world, but from which they, at least, could come and go as they pleased. Few people thought of fairies as either intrinsically good or bad. They were generally believed to be capable of behaviour ranging from one extreme to the other. But it was always considered better to be cautious rather than casual about fairies. They could steal food, if it was left unprotected, and what was worse, they could steal an unbaptised child, and leave a fretful, wizened changeling in its place. It was generally considered prudent to take precautions against such things happening, with the use of charms against the fairy magic, or bribes of milk and food to appease them.

The fairy realm was most commonly thought to be a subterranean world, which the fairies reached through hidden entrances in hills, mountains, rocks and sometimes caves. It was generally thought to be a place filled with light, and with music, for the fairies were skilled musicians. It was a place where time seemed to stand still, or to pass very slowly. It was inaccessible to most human beings, and traditionally, those who did find their way into the fairy realm were unlikely to come out again. If they did, their lives were changed.

Thomas the Rhymer

Thomas the Rhymer is a very 'weel-kent' figure in Scots story-telling and poetry, a man who is believed to have prophesied many major events in Scottish history while he was alive. He was said to speak the truth always, hence the other name by which he is commonly known, True Thomas. Although Thomas the Rhymer is a legendary figure, and is said to have lived in various parts of the country, it is most commonly believed that the legends originally grew up around a poet who lived in the Scottish borders during the thirteenth century. Thomas was born Thomas Learmont of Ercildoune. Ercildoune was a village now known as Earlston, situated in the Scottish border country, not far from the towns of Galashiels and Melrose. According to the most famous legend of his life, Thomas was not born with the gift of prophecy, but acquired it from the queen of the fairies.

Thomas was out walking in the Eildon Hills near his home one day, and he stopped to rest by Huntly Water, under the shade of the Eildon Tree. As he lay half-dozing in the shade, something caught his eye, and he turned to see a beautiful woman, clad in green silk and velvet, riding towards him on a white horse which had a bridle festooned with bright silver bells. There was something extraordinary about this woman, and Thomas was captivated by her beauty. As soon as he caught sight of her, he jumped to his feet, removed his hat and bowed before her. He thought she must be the Queen of Heaven, and addressed her as such. But the woman told him that she was not the Queen of Heaven, but the Queen of Elfland, where the fairies lived. Thomas was surprised to find that she knew his name, but he was even more perplexed when she declared that she had come expressly to seek him out. She dared him to kiss her on the lips, and Thomas did not hesitate. The Queen of Elfland now had him in her power.

'Now,' said the queen, 'you must come with me to Elfinland, where you will serve me for seven years, for good or for bad.'

Thomas was entranced with his new acquaintance and climbed up behind her on the horse without another word. They rode on and on, until they were far from any place familiar to Thomas, and it seemed as if the journey might never end. When the horse finally drew to a halt, the lush, green summer countryside was nowhere to be seen and they were in a barren desert. The Queen dismounted with Thomas.

'Now,' she said, 'I have three wonders to show you.' She pointed to three different roads that lay ahead of them, each going in a different direction. The first road was overgrown with thorns and briars. Travel along such a road would be painful and difficult, for the thorns made it almost impossible to make one's way along it.

'That road,' the Queen told Thomas, 'is the road to Righteousness. There are few men who choose to take it.'

The second road was wide and easy to travel on. Lilies, their heads heavy with scented pollen, grew all along the verges.

'That road,' the Queen said, 'is the road to Hell, although many people do not believe it and mistake it for the road to Heaven.'

The third road stretched ahead through a green landscape, covered in a dense blanket of ferns.

'That road,' said the Queen, 'is the road to Elfinland, where we are going. While you are in Elfinland, Thomas, you must remember one thing. You must never speak. If you utter a single word, you will never be able to return to your own land.'

The Queen and Thomas travelled on into the night. It was a difficult journey, for they had to cross rivers and rocky countryside in the darkness, and there was no moon to light their way. Then they came to a river that was unlike all the others. As they waded through the murky waters, Thomas could just make out that the water was blood red.

'This is the river that carries away all the blood that is shed on the earth,' the Queen told him.

They rode on until at last they game to a garden, which was full of trees laden with fruit of all kinds. The Queen went up to an apple tree and plucked a plump, red fruit from its branches and handed it to Thomas.

'Take this in payment,' she said to him. 'Eat it, and you will have a tongue that can never lie.'

Thomas took the apple from the Queen and ate it, overawed at having been given such a priceless gift.

'Now Thomas,' said the Queen, 'remember, not another word.' Thomas nodded. They mounted the horse and rode on, deep into the fairy realm.

Thomas was given a suit of green clothes and green velvet shoes, and so began his service to the Fairy Queen. The time he spent in Elfinland passed quickly, and it seemed to Thomas that only a few days had gone by when the Queen summoned him to her and told him that he was free to go. But time in Elfinland is not the same as time in the land of the humans, and the Queen told him that when he returned to his own land, he would find that he had been away for seven years. As he took his leave of the Fairy Queen, she bade him a fond farewell, but said that she would see him again.

'I will come again and call you back to Elfinland,' she told him. 'When the day comes, you will know.'

And so Thomas the Rhymer returned to the land of humans, and not a word did he say to anyone of what he has seen and learned during his stay in Elfinland. His reputation as a prophet soon became known far and wide, and the accuracy with which he was able to foretell what would happen in the future was astonishing. He lived a contented life. He was a respected member of the community in which he lived, and his honesty and forthrightness were much appreciated by all those who knew him. He did not know when the day would come for him to return to the Fairy Queen, but he bided his time patiently, knowing that some day, a sign would be given to him.

And so it happened that one day, a young lad came running into the village, saying that he had seen a white hart and a white hind coming out of the forest nearby. Several of the villagers gathered together and went to see if what the boy was saying was true and sure enough, at the edge of the wood, they saw two white deer standing calmly beneath the trees, watching and waiting. The villagers called upon Thomas and told him what they had seen. They wanted to know if the unusual sight was an omen. When Thomas had listened to their news, he smiled, for he knew what it meant, but he did not explain. He simply bade his friends an affectionate farewell and walked off to the edge of the forest where the two creatures stood. Then all three moved off together and disappeared into the trees. Thomas the Rhymer was never seen again.

The Fiddlers of Tomnahurich

There was once a pair of musicians, who lived in Inverness-shire. They were down on their luck, and in spite of their considerable skills in playing the fiddle, had not found an audience to pay them well for a long time. And so it was that when they met an old man who said he could find them a night's work, they gladly took him up on his offer. The old man took the fiddlers up the hill at Tomnahurich, and in through an entrance in the hillside that they had never seen before. They followed him in and the entrance closed behind them. The fiddlers found themselves in a bright place, richly decorated and full of the sound of laughter, where beautiful slender women, handsome men and delicate-featured children were feasting. There was food and drink in abundance, and the two musicians were invited to take their fill before the dancing began. When they had eaten all that they wanted, they tuned up their fiddles and started to play. The dancing went on all night, and the fiddlers had as good a time as the revellers did. When it seemed at last that everyone had had enough, the old man paid them well for their trouble with a bag of gold coins, and ushered them out of the mysterious place into the grey light of dawn.

The fiddlers made their way back down the hillside in fine spirits, but when they got into town they were greatly taken aback by what they saw. New buildings had sprung up here and there, and the place looked completely different. They walked through the town without seeing a soul that they recognised, and that was most unusual. Everyone was dressed very strangely, and several people whom they passed commented on the fiddler's 'old-fashioned' clothing. They heard the church bell ringing, calling people to worship, and decided to seek comfort in the familiar rituals of the church service. They walked into the church and settled themselves in their pew, still puzzled to notice that there was not a familiar face in the congregation. The minister came up to the pulpit and the fiddlers stood up with the other members of the congregation, ready to begin the morning's worship. But when the minister began to speak, and mentioned the name of God, the two fiddlers crumbled to dust.

They had not been away for just one night. They had been kept in the Fairy Realm for one hundred years. And the old man who had invited them inside was none other than Thomas the Rhymer.

giant Lore

The countryside of Scotland is quieter now, for most of the giants are dead, or slumbering beneath the hills on which they used to sit. But in times gone by, the sound of their battles echoed across the glens and the noise made by the missiles that they threw at one another across lochs and estuaries here and there sent fishermen fleeing to the safety of the shores in their boats. These battles were a favourite form of entertainment for the giants. Two rivals, sitting on the tops of adjoining hills, or perched on promontories at either side of a bay, would take it in turns to fling their weapons – boulders, hammers, or great pickaxes – at one another. Sometimes one island-dwelling giant would pick a fight with another, living on another island near to him, and great stones would be hurled across the sea between the two. The giants did little damage to each other, for we are told that the accuracy with which they aimed these missiles left much to be desired. All over Scotland lies a litter of stones that are said to have been left where they fell, after being hurled by one giant at another. Two great boulders, one white and one black, were left on opposite shores of Loch Ness after a feud between two giants who lived near there ended in stalemate. Another giant who lived in Kintail, once tried to hit a rival who lived across the water in Skye. He missed, and the boulder that he flung crashed to the ground near Portree. There are giants' boulders on the east coast and the west, on the shores of the Cromarty Firth and in the Hebrides, in the Grampians, the Cairngorms, the hills of Fife and the Scottish Borders. On Law Hill, by Dundee, the 'De'il's Stane' can be found. It is said that it was thrown across the Tay by a giant from Norman's Law at his rival on Law Hill, but fell short of its mark. At Ben Ledi, overlooking the town of Callander, a more amicable contest took place between a number of giants. A giant who was given the name of Samson lived there, and believing that he was the strongest of all, he challenged all comers to a shot-putting contest. The 'shot' was a boulder of enormous size, which they took it in turns to throw from the summit of Ben Ledi. 'Samson's putting-stone' lies where he last flung it, on the east side of the Ben.

The giants could be a terrible torment to humans, and they were notoriously hard to kill. Traditionally, they could be slain if their vulnerable spot – usually described as a mole – could be found. Otherwise, it took a combination of perseverance, brute strength, ingenuity and magic to kill them.

The Morvern Giant

Long ago, there lived a great giant in Morvern, which is on the west coast of Argyll, between Loch Linnhe and Loch Sunart. Across the sea from Morven, on the Isle of Mull, lived several more giants, whom the Morvern giant disliked intensely. He would often amuse himself by tossing boulders at them, across the Sound of Mull. He was bigger and stronger than any of the Mull giants, and he succeeded in causing one or two of them serious injury, much to his delight. The Morvern giant could pick up a cow or a bullock with one hand, and it made a fine meal for him. The sea provided another source of food for the giant, but of course, there was not a fish big enough to satisfy his appetite. When he went fishing, he was looking for a much bigger catch. His fishing rod was made from a tall, straight, silver birch tree, from which he had torn all the branches and roots. His line had been stolen from some fishermen, and it was the longest, strongest rope that they had. For a hook, the giant used an anchor. He had picked it up from the bottom of the harbour and snapped the rope that tied it to its ship. The ship had floated out into the sea in the middle of the night and had never been seen again. The giant would sit on a hillock by the water at the Point of Ardnamurchan, and cast his great hook and line far out to sea. Then one after another, he would haul great whales in to shore, roaring with laughter as they thudded onto the beach.

The giant was also a thief, and one day he stole some treasure from the king of Ardnamurchan. He did not need to sneak past the guards. He did not have to creep in under cover of darkness. He simply stuck his hand down a chimney and helped himself to all the gold and silver that was lying in the room below.

The king and his men gave chase, which was a very brave thing to do, considering the size and strength of the thief. The giant was heading eastward from the Point of Ardnamurchan, trudging along the northern shore of Loch Sunart, heading for the end. The king and his men knew that when the giant got to the end of the loch, he would turn south and west again, heading for his home in Morvern, and so they got in a boat and crossed Loch Sunart from north to south in order to intercept him. The cries of the king as he urged on his oarsmen alerted the giant to his pursuers. He picked up a great boulder and lifted it high above his head. Then he threw it into the loch, making great waves that tossed the king's boat from side to side like a twig in a torrent. But the king's men would not give up. With tremendous courage and tenacity, they battled through the raging waters to the other side of the loch, just as the giant was making his way up the hillside towards his home. Then the bravest warrior among the king's men called out to the giant, challenging him to stop and fight. The giant laughed, for he knew that he had the strength to crush every one of the king's men with his bare hands. He turned his face towards them, ready to answer the challenge with a scornful sneer. But when the warrior who had shouted out the challenge looked at the giant's face, he saw that there was a red mole right in the middle of his forehead, and knew that this was his weak spot. He drew his bow and, swiftly and surely, shot an arrow at the giant's forehead, hitting him right in the middle of the blemish. With a crash that echoed all across the peninsula, the giant fell dead to the ground. The king's men gathered up the stolen treasure and loaded it onto their boat. Then they cut off the giant's head and rolled it down the hillside to the shore. The weight of their load almost sank their boat as they sailed back over the loch to Ardnamurchan, with the triumphant giant slayer at the helm.

the glaistig and the kelpie

Highland folklore is animated by a wide variety of supernatural creatures, either harmful, or benevolent, and there are countless tales of man's encounters with them, some tragic, some humorous, some romantic. Two such creatures that feature in a large number of stories are the *glaistig* and the *kelpie* (*each-uisge*, or water-horse).

The glaistig was always female, a tutelary being who was believed to dwell in lochs and rivers, and to have a special attachment to animals and young children. When she did make herself visible to the human eye, it was said that she appeared as half-woman, half-goat, or as a woman with long fair hair, clothed in green. She watched over sheep and cattle, saving them from straying into danger. Often, as the adults went about their daily chores, the glaistig kept the children entertained with fun and games. It was commonly thought that glaistigs could attach themselves to particular families, as guardian spirits. In many parts of the Highlands offerings of milk or food were often left out for the glaistig to ensure that her loyalty to those under her protection remained steadfast. There was another side to the glaistig, however. She could tease and torment, and sometimes, she could do harm. The story of the glaistig's curse illustrates this belief.

The kelpie, water-horse or *each uisge*, was another water-dwelling creature. It was widely thought to be malevolent, capable of luring many innocent souls to their deaths in its sub-aquatic lair. Although it was sometimes said to have the power to transform itself into the shape of a man, it generally appeared on land as a magnificent horse and tempted weary travellers to try to ride upon its back. Once they had mounted, they found that they could not dismount and were dragged, helpless, underwater by the kelpie. There they would be devoured. Sometimes evidence could be found of the victim's fate. It was generally thought that the kelpie did not eat all of its victims, but left a small part of them – the liver, some said, or the heart – and these would be washed up at the water's edge where searchers could find them. One story tells of a number of children who encounter a kelpie while playing at the water's edge. All but one of them climb on the creature's back. The last child reaches out to stroke the creature's head, and as his first finger touches it, it becomes stuck fast. The child draws his knife and cuts off his finger in order to save himself but can only stand and watch as his companions disappear beneath the waves on the kelpie's back. In another version of the same story, six little girls are lured on to the kelpie's back, but the seventh child, a boy, is too cautious to risk it. The kelpie tries to catch him, but he manages to escape. Most kelpies appeared as black horses, but the River Spey was thought to be the home of a kelpie that took the form of a great white horse. The deaths of many people who drowned in the river's white-flecked, tumbling waters were blamed upon the kelpie. The majority of stories about kelpies depict this mysterious creature at its worst; a mortal enemy of man, who may sometimes be outwitted, but should always be feared. The story of the Kelpie of Loch Garvie is different.

The Glaistig of Ardnadrochit

There was once a glaistig who lived in Ardnadrochit on the Isle of Mull. She was a guardian of the Lamont family and looked after all the cattle that belonged to them. She was devoted to her duties. One day, as the glaistig was out herding the cattle, she saw some men approaching. They were cattle raiders from Lorne, and they had come to steal the beasts away from her. The glaistig could not move the cattle fast enough to get them to safety, but she would not allow the raiders to take them away. She struck the animals on their backs with her magic wand, and turned them all, one after another, into great grey stones, which are still lying where she left them.

The glaistig had foiled the thieves but the loss of her animals broke her heart and there was nothing that the Lamont family could do to console her. She pined away and died, and they buried her close to the stones.

The Kelpie of Loch Garve

The kelpie of Loch Garve lived in a cold, dark, underwater lair, hidden from sight in the very deepest part of the loch. He liked his home just fine, and although he ventured onto land from time to time, he was always glad to get back to familiar surroundings, where his wife waited for him. But the kelpie's wife was not happy. She felt the cold terribly, and life in the lair was miserable for her as she shivered and shook, trying, and failing to get warm. She complained to her husband, but he did not feel the cold like she did, and at first he thought that she was just making a fuss over nothing. Time went on, and the kelpie's wife became more and more unhappy. At last, he realised that if he wanted to keep her, he would have to do something to make the place a little more comfortable for her. He left home the very next day, and swam to the surface of the loch, where he turned himself into a beautiful horse. Then he went to the house of a man he had heard of, a builder who knew how to construct all sorts of useful things. When he got to the builder's house, he stamped on the ground until the man came out. The builder was surprised to see such a beautiful horse on his doorstep. It seemed to be waiting patiently for him to mount it, and so he climbed on. As soon as the builder was sitting upon his back, the kelpie took off like the wind. The builder was terrified, for he realised that he was stuck fast to the kelpie's back, and they were heading towards the loch. He muttered a silent prayer as the kelpie plunged into the water, and he felt himself going down, down into the cold and dark. But the kelpie did not want to harm him. When they got to the bottom of the loch, he let the builder dismount. Then he explained his problem to him. He told him how his wife could not get warm in their home deep down in the loch, and how unhappy she was. And he asked the builder to help. If the builder could make something to help the kelpie's wife get warm, then he would be able to return safely to dry land, with a promise of a plentiful supply of fish from the loch to eat, whenever he wanted it.

The builder set to work at once, and made a great big fireplace in the kelpie's lair, with a great big chimney to carry the smoke to the surface of the water. When the work was complete, and the fire was lit, the kelpie looked at the smile on his wife's face with pleasure. He returned the builder safely to his own home on dry land, and true to his word, kept the kindly tradesman supplied for the rest of his days with plenty of fine, fresh fish from the loch. They say that even in the coldest of winter weathers, when all around is frozen, there is one small area of water on Loch Garve that stays free from ice. That is because far below the surface, a fire is burning merrily in the kelpie's home, and the heat which rises up from it stops the water on the surface from freezing.

The killing of the kelpie of Raasay

There was once a blacksmith who lived on Raasay. He owned a number of cattle and some sheep, and from time to time, one of the beasts disappeared. The smith knew that the likely culprit was the kelpie who dwelt in the loch nearby. He was angry, but felt that he could do little to stop it happening. Then one day the kelpie went too far. The smith's daughter had been out working with the animals that day, and she did not return home at the usual time. Evening turned into night and still there was no sign of her. The smith waited anxiously for many hours, then as soon as the dawn came up, he went with his son to look for her. When they reached the edge of the loch, they found the girl's liver lying amongst the pebbles and realised at once that the kelpie must have taken her. The smith's fury knew no bounds. He made up his mind to destroy the creature. With the help of his son, he lit a great fire at the water's edge, and used it as a makeshift forge to make a number of large iron hooks. Then the two men set up a spit on which they put a sheep to roast. As the sheep's carcass began to cook, sending an appetising aroma over the waters of the loch, the smith set the hooks in the fire to heat until they were red-hot. The greedy water-horse caught the scent of the cooking meat and surfaced. It swam over to the fire and made a grab for the sheep's carcass with its jaws and as it did so, the smith and his son set about it with the red-hot hooks. At last it was dead, and they turned away, leaving its inert body lying on the shore. The next day, the smith and his son returned to the lochside but could find no trace of the kelpie's body. All that was left by the ashes of the fire was a heap of starshine.

ghostly animals

A faithful pet

Dogs are widely thought to be sensitive to ghosts. The following story, which comes from the west coast of Scotland, tells of a dog with a particular attachment to a ghost.

An elderly crofter was heartbroken when his wife of many years died. His two sons had grown up and now had crofts of their own to manage. The old man found his widowed state particularly lonely and hard to bear. His only company at home was their dog, which his wife had been particularly fond of. The dog pined terribly after the death of its mistress and would not eat for many days afterwards. At one stage the crofter feared that the dog might die, but after some time the beast seemed to rally and returned to its former boisterous self.

The crofter would take the dog onto the hillside every day to give it some exercise. The dog was usually very obedient and stayed close to its master, but one day, some weeks after the death of the crofter's wife, the dog ran off. This was completely out of character. In spite of the crofter's whistles and calls, the dog disappeared. The crofter waited for some time but eventually returned home. Some time later the dog returned.

This was to set a pattern for the coming weeks. Mostly the dog would stay in sight of the crofter when they went out, but every few days it would take off and disappear for as long as an hour.

The old man did not have the energy to run after the dog, but one day he followed at his own pace in the direction the dog had taken. Over the brow of a small hill, he came upon an astonishing sight. There was his dog in the distance, in the company of a familiar figure – the crofter's beloved wife. The crofter stood and watched for some moments, then the figure of his wife faded to nothing. The dog, large as life, came bounding back when the crofter called to it. The two made for home, the crofter happier than he had been for a long time because of what he had seen.

The black dog of tiree

Humans are not the only creatures to return in ghostly form after death. There are plenty of spectral animals to be seen around Scotland, especially dogs. The hounds that howl by the ruins of Buckholme Tower in the Borders inspire fear in those who hear them. Another phantom dog has been heard crashing against a bedroom door in Ballechin House in Perthshire. Tiree has yet another canine ghost.

Tiree is a beautiful island off the west coast of Scotland, blessed with long stretches of silver sand around its shores. On and around one such beach on the northern side of the island a ghostly dog has been seen and heard several times. The dog is large and black and usually makes itself heard first with a strange, hollow-sounding bark. It will follow people along the beach for quite some distance before it disappears into thin air.

The ghost elk

In *Not of This World*, Maurice Fleming cites the tale of a ghostly elk which was seen by Laurence Blair Oliphant, the Laird of Ardblair.

As a small boy, his Lordship saw, in the woods near his house, "this large, red, antlered animal, running through the trees". Because the trees were so closely planted, there was in fact not enough room for such a big beast to run like that nor, come to think of it, did he hear the thunder of hooves.

Years later, his wife reported seeing a similar creature running noiselessly through the very same stretch of woodland.

It was only later even than that that they realised the animal they had seen was an elk, which used to roam the Great Caledonian Forest, alongside the wolves and bears which are also now extinct in Scotland.

scottish witches

a charmed Life:
superstition and witchcraft

Whether or not we admit to being superstitious, there are few of us who do not pay some sort of homage to superstitious practices and beliefs – we might cross our fingers or touch wood, for example, throw spilled salt over our left shoulder, or have in our possession 'lucky' items of clothing, coins, stones or talismans.

Superstitious behaviour is almost as old as man and is practised in societies in every corner of the globe. As man has struggled to forge a living in a world he does not fully understand, and against elements and occurrences over which he has little or no control, he has sought to explain the inexplicable through beliefs in external, unworldly forces; to predict the unpredictable and to control the uncontrollable through practices aimed at manipulating good and evil towards his own ends; appeasing the forces that might work against him, nurturing the forces that could benefit him.

In Scottish culture there is a great wealth of customs, sayings and actions that have accumulated through centuries of superstitious belief, and many of which are still practised by people today. Some people will still plant rowan trees, believed to provide protection against evil spirits, outside their homes. When a mother takes her new baby out for the first time, neighbours and friends might still place silver coins in the prams of new infants, for giving a gift to a newborn child, especially one of silver, is thought to bring both the giver and the child good fortune. But when can a superstitious practice be considered a spell, or a charm of witchcraft?

Witchcraft is believed to invest the practising individual with certain powers, whilst superstitious practices offer protection. Sometimes, moreover, the protection sought through superstitious practices is against the perceived evils that witches might be believed to cause. However, the two are still strongly tied to each other – they have much in common. Talismans, symbols, incantations or sayings, rituals – these are elements shared by witchcraft and superstition. It is not always clear which is which. When we see a solitary magpie and politely wish it 'good morning' to avert ill-fortune, are we merely being superstitious, or are we casting a spell?

When Christianity was introduced to Scotland, superstition was already deeply rooted, and the practice of magic already hundreds of years old. And whilst Christianity dismissed the pagan gods from the converted people's minds, it did not altogether supersede superstition. Nor did it entirely dispel beliefs in magic. Indeed, it can be argued that superstition continued to exist quite comfortably alongside Christianity in Scotland. Some of our superstitions, such as avoiding having thirteen guests seated at the same table, have their origins in the Christian religion. Many old Scottish traditional practices carried out in the celebration of milestones in life, or special festivals, combined religious belief with an abiding indulgence in superstition. For example, in some parts of Scotland, where a boy and a girl were both presented for baptism on the same day, the girl had to be baptised first. If the boy's baptism were to precede the girl's, it was believed that the girl might grow a beard in later life. There were careful precautions taken for the protection of new-born infants, and certain procedures to be followed around the time of their birth, to prevent them from being taken away by fairies. When a death had taken place an equal number of precautions were taken to ensure that the spirits of the newly dead were protected from the forces of evil until a proper funeral sent them safely into the afterlife. In times gone by it was not necessarily considered enough to put your trust in God for protection against malign forces.

With the advent of Christianity, the role of the practitioners of magic gradually changed over the centuries, both in their own eyes and in the eyes of others. As far as the authorities of the Christian Church were concerned, witchcraft was heresy.

Like superstition and witchcraft, religion has its rituals, symbols, incantations and over time, we find that witches in Scotland began to integrate some elements of Christian services or prayers, albeit in adapted form, into their own practice. After the Reformation in Scotland, when the practice of Roman Catholicism was abhorred by so many leading Protestants, practitioners of magic frequently found they were considered guilty of a twofold heresy – i.e. practising witchcraft and acknowledging the rites of Roman Catholicism. Witches still commonly used, or misused, elements of the Roman Catholic mass in their rituals and charms. The idea of the Demonic pact – that witches had actively renounced their baptism and transferred their allegiances to Satan – was one which is thought to have originated in Europe and influenced Scottish witch-beliefs in the late sixteenth and early seventeenth centuries. Charges laid against accused witches and the confessions of the accused themselves, reflected how this belief had become practice. Along with the idea of the Demonic pact came that of the sabbat. Although the sabbat of the 'black' witches was not a true subversion of the Christian mass, it would frequently be conducted on sacred ground, and the prayers and incantations recited by many witches, whether these be 'white', healer witches or 'black' witches whose practice was largely malevolent and who admitted to being active devotees of Satan, frequently contained elements from, or were little more than adulterated versions of prayers that were commonly recited in the pre-Reformation Christian church.

Gradually, scepticism regarding the effectiveness and hence, the real threat of witchcraft began to overtake the fear. Whilst the church authorities might still rail against the witches as heretics and enemies God, the law makers and enforcers gradually came to the conclusion that connections like those which had been made in past years between misfortune and witchcraft were spurious, and that the practice of witchcraft itself, unless accompanied by physical violence, could not cause physical harm or death. In short, whatever the intent of the witch, whether good or evil, witchcraft did not work, and people could not commit crimes using witchcraft alone. Accordingly, the crime of witchcraft was removed from the statute books.

The period of the witch-hunts did not stamp out witchcraft in Scotland. Superstition and witchcraft alike had already shown themselves to be adaptable to change. They had modified over the centuries to absorb the influences of changing religious beliefs and practices, and of foreign witch beliefs and superstitions. In the centuries since the witch hunts, witchcraft has continued, and whilst elements of traditional magic are retained, it still continues to evolve, incorporating a fluid and changing variety of beliefs and practices into its whole.

wicca and modern witchcraft

Wicca is a modern attempt to reconstruct what its followers believe is the world's oldest religion - witchcraft. This religion finds its origins in northern Europe and is centred on a belief in a fertility goddess, sometimes known as the Earth Mother or even May Queen, and her consort, the God of the Hunt, also known as the Green Man.

Despite this connection with the distant past, Wiccans are generally under no illusions that their "craft" is anything other than a modern take on an old faith, much of which was systematically wiped out by the early Christian movement.

That Wicca should emerge in the late 1940s after, perhaps thousands of years of lying pretty much dormant can be partially attributed to the increasingly secular nature of our society from the Industrial Revolution onwards.

That, and the advent of a series of writings that once again sparked people's interest in a long-lost religion promising a closer understanding of the natural world and a way of living in peace at a time when, all around, the world was at war.

Margaret Murray's books, including *The Witch Cult of Western Europe* and *The God of the Witches*, published in the early decades of the twentieth century, put forward the idea that the witches who were persecuted in the 16th and 17th centuries were not the unfortunate victims of mass hysteria so much as occasional practitioners of a much earlier, comprehensive pan-European religion.

Most historians laughed in her face but her works endured.

Whatever enthusiasm Murray may have ignited was fanned into flame by Gerald Gardner, a civil servant and Wiccan coven member who published several books detailing Wicca's origins, beliefs, rituals and concepts.

It was he who first related modern witchcraft to the ancient worship of the fertility goddess and her consort. He went on to describe Wicca as a religion whose rituals related to the moon.

Wiccans celebrate the full moons and sometimes also the new moons, as well as the spring and autumn equinoxes. Curiously, Druidic worship, which must have existed at the same time, centred itself on the activities of the sun, which Druids believed was hugely powerful and no less than the bestower of life.

Gardner claimed, controversially, that the link between ancient and modern witchcraft had never been broken. Many others then and since dispute this, insisting that modern witchcraft is a restoration based on the fragments of information and ritual that were not extinguished by churches, and incorporating elements of other belief systems, including rituals taken from the Masonic Order and ceremonial magic.

Wiccan beliefs and rites

Wiccans believe ...

1   ... that the divine can be seen in everything, from a blade of grass to a shower of rain to a child's smile. They are not concerned with demonic rituals and calling up the devil, and are hence also known as white witches. Instead, they concentrate their energies on healing, teaching, learning and offering protection against malevolent forces.

2   ... in the three-fold system, also known as the "law of three", whereby anything that they put out into the world will return to them threefold. This, as you can imagine, works as a very powerful disincentive to using Wicca to perpetrate evil or cause harm to others. In fact, Wicca is a very reflective religion in which practitioners are encouraged to consider the import of everything they do, and how it impacts on others.

3   ...in a god, or single deity, whom they consider to be "unknowable". The fertility goddess and her consort are seen less as deities and more as intermediaries between earth and a higher realm. However, most prayers are issued to these two figures, rather than directly to the deity.

   Thus, some Wiccans can reconcile their practice of modern witchcraft with a Christian faith.

   Wicca rituals include baptisms, though in this case the child is not committed to the religion. Indeed, Wiccans only accept members aged 18 or over, when they are sufficiently mature to exercise an independent and informed decision, and an adult baptism is enacted.

Wiccans also have their own marriage ceremonies.

4   ... that, as long as you harm no-one else, you can do as you wish. This is known as the Wiccan Rede, and relates to the Wiccan idea of personal responsibility.

Spells, for instance, should not be constructed so as to force anyone to do anything, as this violates the Wiccan Rede's invocation against manipulation and control. So if you are in the market for a love potion or to have a rival turned into a toad, you will need to look somewhere else.

In fact, Wicca does not have a set repertoire of spells though Wiccans may contruct ones which, for instance, would help a lonely person become more open to love, or a jealous person find solace through something more positive than revenge.

5   ... in sexual equality and tolerance of sexualities, including homosexuality and bisexuality.

6   ... in the reincarnation of the human soul. Rather than the heaven and hell system of Christian faiths. Wiccans, like Celts, believe that life and death are part of the same, endless cycle and that the dead should be revered, not feared.

Though Wicca is a recognised religion, it is not easy to access as covens are not listed in phone directories the way regular religious organisations are. The best way to contact them is through word-of-mouth, or by attending pagan festivals where you should be able to get talking to like-minded individuals. But non-Wiccans are warned, as with Mediums, to check a person/ group's credentials before committing themselves.

Though Wicca remains a little elusive, it has hit the headlines recently, when Scotland became the location of the first authorised Wiccan wedding.

Paul Rickards and Louise Schender, from Canada, were married in 2004 in a Wiccan ceremony held in Edinburgh's underground vaults and conducted by the Niddry Street Temple of the Source Coven of the Blue Dragon, by George Cameron and Lady Felina, the coven's High Priest and High Priestess.

Commenting, a spokesperson for the General Registry Office of Scotland said: "It is the first Wicca wedding to be authorised in Scotland. It is a recommended form of religion. The Registrar General for Scotland attaches great importance to the principle of marriage."

As did the happy couple who, though not practising Wiccans, found the belief system on which it is based very much to their taste.

white witches

There are other "categories" of white witches still practising today, some of which are as follows:

Kitchen witches

Kitchen Witches have more in common with herbalists than Wiccans in that their witchery is very much focussed on the utilisation of herbs and plants for healing and restorative purposes. They also tap into earth energies and the elements of fire, wind and water, and base their activities round the kitchen hearth, hence their generic name. They are sometimes referred to as Green Witches.

Hereditary witches

Some practising witches claim to have inherited their knowledge and skills from family members, who passed this lore down through the generations. Many such were wiped out during the time of the witch-trials, when such knowledge was viewed more as a curse than a blessing. Many others dropped the familial tradition, believing it flew in the face of Christianity.

Eclectic or solo witches

Eclectic or Solo Witches do not belong to a coven or work according to an established set of beliefs. Instead, they prefer to work alone, picking and choosing whatever elements of witchcraft work best for them.

Correllian nativist tradition

Unlike other forms of modern witchcraft, the Correllian Nativist Tradition, which is based on Wicca incorporating beliefs and rituals from Native American religions, favour the idea of Wicca operating on a worldwide, organised basis rather than through isolated groups. To this end, they have established a unified tradition with a single leadership. They pride themselves on their accessibility and are great promoters of Wiccan education, even offering correspondence courses via the internet.

Dianic tradition

Dianic Witches belong to female-only covens and devote themselves only to the goddess of fertility. They have similarities with the Dryadic Witches, another female-only sect, who draw much of their ideas and beliefs from fairy lore.

pagan festivals

As church attendance continues to decline in Scotland, one area where religious observation appears to be on the up is in Paganism, which has many similarities with Wicca in that it is centred around the natural world and is essentially benign, concerned with doing good not evil.

Pagans celebrate eight major festivals a year, at six to seven week intervals, giving the year a rhythmic structure. This structure is known as the Wheel of the Year, which accords with the Wiccan idea of life being, in essence, circular.

Imbolc (February 1 or 2)

Imbolc is also known as the day of Bride, the goddess of fire, and Pagans mark it by lighting fires to hasten the return of the sun after the long winter so as to ensure that the spring planting goes well.

It is a time when many attend to domestic tasks, such as sweeping out the house – the basis of our modern-day concept of spring cleaning – and making candles.

Imbolc was assimilated into the Christian calendar, becoming Candlemass, where candles are lit to honour the purity and holiness of the Virgin Mary.

Spring Equinox (March 20 or 21)

This is the day when spring officially begins, as the length of the day now equals that of the night. Christianity appropriated this one too, turning it into Easter, the celebration of the Resurrection and incorporating many Pagan rituals associated with the idea of birth and regeneration, such as egg painting and seed planting.

Beltane (April 30 or May 1)

This is the great fire festival to welcome in the summer. Fire, to the Pagans, is linked to fertility and purity and many love matches were sealed at this time of year. Mayday, celebrated particularly in England, typifies Beltane's delight in sexuality and fecundity.

In Edinburgh, Beltane attracts thousands of people to Calton Hill every April 30, where fires are lit and crowds gather to watch the May Queen arrive with the Green Man. The Queen crowns him, after which he sheds his winter clothes and they both get married.

Lughnasadh (August 1 or 2)

Like Lammas, or the loaf mass, this is a harvest thanksgiving essentially, celebrated with singing, dancing and feasting. It is also a time for prudence, and for making plans for the winter.

Autumn Equinox (September 20 or 21)

The equinox marks the end of summer and is a time for reflection.

Samhain (October 31 or November 1)

This is the beginning of the Pagan year, when gods or spirits were thought to roam the earth, mingling with human beings. This undoubtedly gave rise to Hallowe'en, which is characterised as a wild night when the spirits rise again, before scurrying away in the face of All Saints' Day on 1st November.

Pagans celebrated with feasting and dancing. However, many modern Pagans are vegetarians, factory-farming having little correlation with a holistic view of man and animals, and the kind of drunkenness associated with ancient rituals is often foregone too.

Winter Solstice (December 22)

This is the shortest day of the year, when the sun "dies" at sunset, only to be reborn the following morning, marking the "return of the sun". Rituals included gathering at sacred sites to watch the sun go down, and lighting a Yule Log – a log that burned for days – to banish the darkness.

Many other traditions grew from this, including that of Father Winter, a rather malevolent old man who wandered from house to house, demanding to be entertained. If he was turned away, he would stick around, ensuring the winter was perpetual. He was later sanitised, with a little help from St Nicholas, into our modern day Santa Claus.

the hunted

In sixteenth- and seventeenth-century Scotland any distinction between 'white' and 'black' magic became irrelevant, and any notion of magic working independently of either God or the Devil was dismissed. The practice of magic was the work of the Devil, God's greatest foe. Curing, harming, charming, cursing, foretelling the future and talking to spirits of the dead were equally suspect activities. Those who claimed to do any such things, those who were seen to do any such things, and those who were said to have done any such things were equally liable to find themselves in danger from the wrath of the church authorities and the courts.

What was a witch, in the eyes of those who led the witch hunts of the sixteenth and seventeenth centuries? Who were these people who were persecuted in their hundreds?

The statistics that can be calculated from surviving records of witch trials reveal, to a certain extent, certain factors that were held in common by a significant number of the accused.

Firstly, although men were prosecuted for witchcraft, it is true to say that the majority of those who were tried for such crimes were women. Throughout the period of witch persecutions, around 80 per cent of those suspected of witchcraft were female. This is sometimes interpreted as sign of women's inferior status in society, or of 'institutional misogyny' on the part of the church and the courts. But the figures may simply illustrate social perceptions of witchcraft at the time; it was seen primarily as a woman's crime. That is to say, because of the things that people believed to be true about witches, women were more likely suspects, and therefore more women were apprehended.

The age of a 'typical' Scottish witch is not so easy to tell. Some were old, some were little more than girls, but there are indications that the majority of those who were accused were in the 'middle-age' bracket. Most were married, or widowed, and were therefore clearly adults. Several had children, many of whom were adults themselves. There were certainly several old women who found themselves on trial for witchcraft during the period, but any notion of the typical Scottish witch of the sixteenth and seventeenth centuries being a wizened old hag would be wrong.

If there is one thing that can be said to be true of all the alleged witches who were prosecuted in Scotland in the sixteenth and seventeenth centuries, whether they saw themselves as witches or not, it is perhaps that they were all people who (through their own fault or otherwise) found themselves with enemies, and who then fell foul of a belief that pervaded all ranks of society at the time: the belief that witchcraft entailed real and *effective* practices, that could be used for good or for evil. Had that belief not been as prevalent as it was, whether they were innocent of practising witchcraft or guilty, these people could never have been successfully prosecuted in such large numbers. Had that belief not been as prevalent as it was, we might argue that it is unlikely that the Witchcraft Act of 1563 would ever have been passed.

two famous witch trials

The North Berwick Witches

The story of the North Berwick witch trials deserves to be singled out for special attention for a number of reasons. It was the first mass witch-trial to take place in Scotland and is notable for the numbers of people who were alleged, in the confessions of those who had been apprehended, to have been taking part in witchcraft in the area around East Lothian. The case also quickly achieved notoriety, even in those cruel times, for the manner in which some of those who were charged suffered for the accusations that had been made against them. The charges that were laid against the people accused of sorcery at North Berwick, and the confessions that were given by some of these people, not only demonstrate quite clearly how hard it is to distinguish the difference between fantasy and fact in cases of this nature, but also bring in an element that had not featured in previous witch trials in Scotland. This was the notion that the persons involved had been taking part in ceremonies and rites in which the Devil was said to have appeared; they had been consorting with and acting directly upon the wishes and demands of Satan himself.

Mention was made, for the first time in a Scottish witch trial, of the Satanic Pact, which swiftly became a major factor in establishing guilt in later prosecutions.

The North Berwick trials were also unique because of the personal part that King James VI played in the investigations and because the events that lead up to the trials involved two countries, Denmark and Scotland. Finally, but not least importantly, the trials of the North Berwick witches are particularly notable because the accused were charged not only with sorcery, but with treason, and the involvement of one of the accused, Francis Stewart, Earl of Bothwell, has been the subject of much debate amongst historians in the years that have passed since.

King James VI had chosen a wife for himself; the fourteen year-old Anne of Denmark. She was to be brought over to Scotland to marry him in 1589, but a succession of storms prevented the boat that was to bring her from setting sail. The Danish authorities blamed witchcraft for the unfortunate weather and consequently a number of people were arrested and brought to trial in Copenhagen. Eventually, King James agreed in the autumn of 1589 to travel overseas to Denmark to meet his betrothed and bring her back to Scotland himself. After a stay of some six months he returned with Anne, now his wife, to Scotland. His journey had been successfully accomplished, but it had been hampered by bad weather, both on the outward and return voyages. On the return voyage one of his ships, carrying wedding gifts for the new queen, was sunk.

In the closing weeks of 1690, the king received some disturbing news. It seemed that the evil that had hindered his marriage plans was not only to be found in Denmark. In his own land, witchcraft and treason were afoot. In North Berwick, a fishing port on the east coast of Scotland, a coven of witches had been working against the king, trying to cause his death through sorcery. The discovery had come to light in the following manner.

Suspicion had fallen first on a woman from Tranent, a servant of David Seton called Geillis Duncan, whose behaviour had caused her master some concern. The rather gruesome pamphlet *'Newes from Scotland'* published in 1591, described how the first suspicions were raised as follows:

'Within the towne of Trenent, in the kingdome of Scotland, there dwelleth one David Seaton who, being deputie bailiffe in the said towne, had a maid called Geillis Duncane, who used secretlie to absent and lie forth of hir maisters house every other night: This Geillis Duncan tooke in hand to helpe all such as were troubled or grieved with anie kinde of sicknes or infirmitie, and in short space did perfourme many matters most miraculous; which things, for asmuch as shee began to do them upon a sodaine, having never done the like before, made her maister and others to be in great admiration, and wondered thereat: by meanes whereof, the said David Seaton had his maid in great suspition that shee did not those things by naturall and lawfull waies, but rather supposed it to bee done by some extraordinarie and unlawfull meanes.'

So far, then, Geillis was not obviously guilty of malefice. She kept disappearing at night, and she seemed to have a new and inexplicable ability to heal the sick. But if she could heal people, then she must also be capable of harm. On Seton's orders, Geillis was tortured – in all likelihood illegally – and examined for the Devil's mark, which was found on her neck. Following interrogation she confessed to having acted with others. More people were apprehended for investigation and over a relatively short space of time, a large number of names were produced, including the following: Agnes Sampson from Haddington, Agnes Thompson from Edinburgh, Doctor Fian from Prestonpans; the wife of George Motts from Lothian; Robert Grierson; Janet

Sandilands, a potter's wife, a smith, Euphame Macalyean, Barbara Napier and several others from Edinburgh and East Lothian.

Agnes Sampson was the oldest and she was brought before King James himself for examination. She refused to give in to questioning and accordingly His Majesty ordered that she be taken to prison to be examined for the telltale mark of a witch and tortured until she confessed. The Devil's mark was found, and after suffering terrible tortures at the hands of her interrogators, Agnes admitted that she was a witch. She was brought in front of the king once more, and this time willingly told him about the treacherous and devilish deeds of which she and her accomplices were guilty. On Hallowe'en, 1589, she and several others had sailed in sieves, drinking and carousing all the way, to North Berwick. Dr Fian had taken the lead in the procession, with Geillis Duncan playing her jew's harp as musical accompaniment. The assembly of witches had danced their way towards the kirk, singing. This story was to be confirmed by Geillis Duncan, who was brought before King James to play her instrument for him to hear.

At the gathering in North Berwick, none other than Satan himself had been present. He had ordered that the king should be killed, and in a strange ceremony which had entailed the removal of joints from bodies buried within and without the kirkyard, the assembled persons had agreed to his wishes, sealing their promise by kissing the Devil's buttocks.

The king initially had strong misgivings about the reliability of Agnes Sampson's confession. He called her a liar. But Agnes, apparently, having previously refused so vehemently to give up a confession, was now quite eager to prove her guilt. She whispered in King James' ear the words that he had exchanged with his wife on their wedding night. Now would he believe that she was a witch? Of course he would.

The meeting at North Berwick might have been the largest meeting – accounts vary, but somewhere between forty and two hundred people were said to have attended – but it had not been the only one, according to the growing testimonies of various of the accused. At one other meeting, Dr Fian, Robert Grierson, Agnes Sampson and others had gone out to sea and had thrown a cat, delivered by the hand of Satan, into the water to try to prevent the king's ship from arriving safely back in Scotland. At another, with the Devil present, a stolen picture of the king was passed from hand to hand and trouble wished upon him. At another meeting, a wax likeness of King James VI was produced. And on yet another occasion, venom from a toad which had been hung upside-down was mixed with urine and 'the thing in the forehead of a new-foaled foal' in an oyster-shell, ready to be left where it might fall upon the king and bring about his destruction.

Agnes Sampson, who had a reputation as a practising witch before the trial, was acknowledged in both age and status as the most senior of the women who were accused. She calmly gave long and detailed accounts of the witches' treasonable and maleficent activities, but her compliance did not bring her any benefits. She was strangled and burnt.

Dr Fian, the Prestonpans schoolmaster, proved to be equally forthcoming under torture and interrogation. He was generally acknowledged as the Devil's clerk in the proceedings at North Berwick – no doubt because he was one of the most educated among the gathering. He gave further information about the meeting at North Berwick kirk. It transpired he had a reputation as a womaniser and as a sorcerer and evidence was offered up by others against him to this effect. Shortly after his confession had been secured, Fian escaped. He was caught again and in spite of his protests that his confession had been false, after further torture he faced the same fate as several of his co-accused.

Barbara Napier was a well-connected woman. Her husband, Archibald Douglas, was a respected citizen of Edinburgh. Her brother-in-law was an advocate. She admitted a connection with Richard Graham, one of the other accused, confessing that she had used his services as a magician on one occasion. She also admitted that she had had similar contact with Agnes Sampson. But throughout the entire proceeding, she denied taking part in any of the treasonable activities of which she had been accused. She had consulted witches, she said; but she was not guilty of practising witchcraft herself. She was initially cleared of the charge of treason, but following the intervention of the king, she was finally found guilty and executed.

Like Barbara Napier, Euphame Macalyean was a member of the Edinburgh gentry; the illegitimate daughter of one advocate, the wife of another. The accusations against her not only involved her alleged participation in the activities of the North Berwick witches, but also her alleged conspiracy to kill her first husband with witchcraft and her use of witchcraft in matters of love and personal dispute. In spite of a powerful legal defence, Euphame Macalyean was found guilty and burned alive.

Richard Graham, another of the accused, also had a reputation as a sorcerer. He was already an excommunicate. He was acknowledged as one of the most powerful figures in the group and may even have been the leader. It was he who commanded Geillis Duncan to assemble with the other witches at North Berwick. He was acquainted with several members of the Scottish nobility who were said to have recognised and at times made use of his magical powers. He confessed to having 'raised the Devil' on more than one occasion. Graham survived longer than most of the other accused, but he, too was eventually executed in 1592.

The confessions of Agnes Sampson, Geillis Duncan, Richard Graham and others all named Francis Stewart, the Earl of Bothwell as the man behind their attempts to kill the king. Bothwell was a powerful figure in Scotland, and had been one of the members of the Regency Council in charge of Scottish affairs while James was away in Denmark, but his relationship with the king was not a comfortable one and it was believed by many that he did indeed pose a threat to the king's security. Whether he had been the figure behind all the intrigue, or whether the allegations of his involvement in the affair were prompted, or manufactured by his political enemies will never be known. He did acknowledge that Richard Graham was known to him, but strenuously denied any part in a magical conspiracy against the king. And whilst proceedings against the other accused moved quite swiftly to a conclusion (although Richard Graham was not executed until 1592, most of those who had been found guilty had been executed by spring 1591), Bothwell's case was to occupy the king's mind for considerably longer. Richard Graham had told in his confession of several meetings which had taken place at which he and Bothwell had discussed how best the king's death might be caused by enchantment. During his period of imprisonment, he also claimed that Bothwell had sent him money in an attempt to bribe him into keeping silent about any such activities.

Bothwell was eventually arrested in May 1591 and imprisoned in Edinburgh Castle. He had several points to bring up in his own defence: Graham was an unreliable witness, as were the other witches who had named him; Graham had been persuaded to make the allegations against him with promises of avoiding execution. But by June, James had been convinced that Bothwell was guilty of treasonable conspiracy, and plans were made to send him into exile abroad. Bothwell foiled the king's plans to send him out of harm's way, however, for he managed to escape and went north into hiding. The king had him declared a traitor and his goods were forfeited to the crown, but Bothwell remained at liberty for two more years, tormenting King James in mind and, on one occasion, threatening him in person at Holyrood Palace. Finally, in 1593, he was brought to trial. King James was not to see Bothwell brought to justice on this occasion either, however, for Bothwell maintained his innocence. His case rested principally on Graham's proven reputation as a sorcerer and hence his unreliability as a witness, and on the claim that Graham had been coerced into manufacturing evidence against him. Bothwell was not short of powerful supporters and few people were surprised when he was acquitted of the charges against him.

It is quite likely that there was a conspiracy to kill King James in 1589–90, and that those who took part in it sought to achieve their ends through the use of black magic. Just how much of the confessions of Agnes Sampson, John Fian, Geillis Duncan and others can be taken as fact will never be known. If everything that was laid against those that were accused is to believed, then the conspiracy was certainly far-reaching. From Edinburgh, to Prestonpans, to North Berwick, there were groups of people from all walks of life who had some part in the affair. Just how many people really were involved will also remain a mystery, for although we know the fates of the more notable figures in the case, we do not know how many others were apprehended and tried for their alleged role in the sorry business.

The role of the Devil in the witches' activities continues to invite speculation. Was this one individual coordinating all efforts, appearing to the witches in demonic guise? Might it have been different men (for the Devil appeared in the form of a man) on different occasions – Richard Graham on one occasion, someone else on others. Or might it even have been Bothwell himself? Did Bothwell instigate the whole affair, or were the allegations of his involvement the result of his enemies, or more specifically, supporters of the king, conspiring to put him out of harm's way? Did Agnes Sampson, Richard Graham and the others who named Bothwell, willingly volunteer Bothwell's name or was it suggested to them? Bothwell was known as a loose cannon, to say the least, and had already been involved in rebellion against the king before 1589. He did know Richard Graham, and had even made use of Graham's skills as a sorcerer in the past. Might he have called upon Graham to help him to get rid of the king and throw the country into chaos? If so, why? Historians are likely to be intrigued by the case for years to come.

The Witches of Pittenweem

By the turn of the eighteenth century, prosecutions for witch-craft were becoming increasingly rare. But in the East Neuk of Fife, in the fishing village of Pittenweem, it appears that witch-fever had not yet burned out.

In 1704, a young boy called Patrick Morton, an apprentice blacksmith who lived in Pittenweem, fell foul of the ill-temper of a woman called Beatrix Laing. She had asked him to make some nails for her, but he had been unable to oblige immediately, his time being taken up with another job on which he was already working. Beatrix took umbrage at his refusal and went away, muttering under her breath. At this point, it seems that the lad's imagination began to take over. He feared that Beatrix was cursing him. Shortly afterwards, when he saw Beatrix tipping hot embers into a bucket of water, he became convinced that she was uttering charms to herself, and assumed that the charms were against him. Some days later, the lad fell ill. He was struck by some mysterious weakness, followed by paralysis and fitting. His body became alarmingly swollen, his head turned to an awkward angle, and he had difficulty breathing. Whatever illness it might have been that

Patrick Morton was suffering from, he believed it had been caused by Beatrix Laing. She had bewitched him. He confided his fears to the local minister, Patrick Cowper, and along with Beatrix Laing, he accused another woman called Janet Cornfoot.

Beatrix Laing was the wife of a respectable burgess of the town. Her husband had served as treasurer of the council. But her position in society was not enough to offer her any protection against Patrick Morton's accusations. It is quite possible that she had already been suspected of witchcraft. She was taken into custody for the process of interrogation to begin. The minister Patrick Cowper, eager to have his conviction, proved to be a cruel tormentor and Beatrix was denied sleep for five days, and subjected to torture. At length, the poor woman gave her interrogators the confession they wanted, naming, as she did so, certain other people, including Janet Cornfoot, Isobel Brown and Nicol Adam. Once her torment had come to an end, however, Beatrix withdrew her confession, on the grounds that it had been obtained under unreasonable duress. This did her no good, for she was subjected to further abuse and then thrown into a dungeon, where she stayed for a period of five months while Cowper made application to have her, and others among her co-accused, tried in Edinburgh. Her case never came to trial in the High Court. It seems that, in Edinburgh, reason prevailed and the Privy Council decided against taking the matter any further. Beatrix was ordered to pay a fine and was released. But justice (or justice as he saw it) was still uppermost in the mind of the minister and good citizens of Pittenweem, and upon Beatrix Laing's release, with the blessings of Mr Cowper, an angry mob hounded her out of her home town.

Isobel Adam was also forced to confess, but she too, in spite of her confession, was able to secure her freedom after payment of a fine. Her fate thereafter is not known, but it is reasonable to assume, in the light of Beatrix Laing's treatment, that she, too, found herself banished from the community.

Another of those who had been apprehended, one of the people whom Isobel Adam named in her confession, was a man called Thomas Brown. He died while in prison in Pittenweem – in all probability his death occurred as a direct result of his treatment while in custody.

Of all those who were accused, Janet Cornfoot suffered the most terribly. She was apprehended following Patrick Morton's accusations, tortured and detained for trial. When, along with that of Beatrix Laing, her case was referred to Edinburgh, she was also released, but she was immediately taken into custody in Pittenweem again. Patrick Cowper was determined that she be re-tried and found guilty. The minister must have had a sadistic streak, for he took it upon himself personally to administer the harshest of floggings, in order to force a confession from her. For a short time, it seemed as if Janet might yet be able to save her own life, for somehow, she managed to escape from prison. But as soon as the news of her escape spread through the town, a frantic search was begun, and before long, the terrified creature was found, dragged out from hiding and hauled down to the beach by a raging mob of townsfolk, baying for her blood. All thoughts of true justice had deserted the people of Pittenweem and Janet's neighbours had become her lynch-mob.

Janet's hands and feet were tied, then she was strung onto a rope stretching between a ship in the harbour and the crowd on the shore. Swinging her outstretched body from side to side, the mob hurled stones at her. When the novelty of this had worn off, they untied her and dumped her, battered and bruised, on the shore. Then they placed a heavy door on top of her, piling boulder upon boulder onto the door until all signs of life in Janet's crushed body were finally extinguished. The good minister and the lawmen did nothing to prevent the horror.

The case of the Pittenweem witches is a particularly horrific episode in the history of the Scottish witch-hunts. The records are full of accounts of ill-treatment, cruelty and injustice, but this stands alone as an example of the terrible consequences of mob hysteria. It is all the worse for the fact that the events took place at a time when in most other parts of Scotland, reason was beginning to prevail. In only thirty years' time, the crimes of which Janet Cornfoot and Beatrix Laing had been accused would no longer be recognised in law.

second sight, prophecies and curses

If those of Celtic blood are more likely to be gifted with psychic "sensitivity" then surely it follows that they are also more likely to be blessed with "second sight"?

One of the most celebrated of all seers, Kenneth Mackenzie, more familiarly known as the Brahan Seer, hailed from these shores, setting an almost unsurpassable precedent for generations of seers to come.

Maybe it is in the genes. Tradition has it that second sight, called *Da Shealladh* in Gaelic (lit. "two sights"), is passed down through the tentacles of families like a curious heirloom, or gifted by a supernatural source for one lifetime only.

Then again, perhaps it is down to the land itself, to the fact that even now many people live in isolated communities, at the mercy of the land, and are still bound together by the old ways of life and the old legends and stories that attach themselves to them.

Maybe the ability to divine the future is part of this stock of ancient lore, an ability we all once had but have lost as our civilisation has progressed towards modernity? Certainly it seems that divination thrives amongst those who live close to the land and away from the cut and thrust of contemporary, urban life.

Most prophecies relate to death, with shrouds and bodies being the most commonly cited visions.

One typical case was recorded by a Rev Dr Stewart, of Nether Lochaber, who was visited by one of his women parishioners who bade him look at a rock by the sea. This rock appeared to be glowing, as if illuminated by phosphorescence. He assumed this odd visual effect was produced through some natural agency but his visitor was adamant that it foretold a death, and said a body would be laid on that spot by nightfall tomorrow.

The next day, a boat arrived bearing a dead body for burial.

The corpse, as the woman parishioner had predicted, was laid at the foot of the rock.

Many books have been written on the subject of second sight, notably the Rev Mr Kirk's *The Secret Commonwealth*, of 1691, which was later edited by no less than Sir Walter Scott. Even such a notable diarist as Samuel Pepys was fascinated by the subject, attempting at one stage to produce a quasi-scientific analysis of it.

However, though a subject of great interest, second sight was not something that people readily owned up to. One reason being that, so legend has it, if you speak out a prophecy before it happens, you lose the ability to see the future! Which just goes to show that the best predictions really are those we hear about afterwards.

Another reason for reticence was the punishment meted out to those who foretold things people did not want to hear.

Though the ability to see into the future is one that has always been envied and highly prized, seers, particularly in the past, have often had less than an easy time of it. Many were blamed for the messages of doom they sometimes had to impart, others were accused of witchcraft or sorcery, still others were written off as deranged.

Thankfully, these days we have a more tolerant attitude towards those who can look into the future and read us our fortune.

Though there are thousands of unattributed tales of people foreseeing deaths and crop failures and famines, only two visionaries have stood the test of time, one ancient the other modern, and their stories are as follows.

the brahan seer

The gift of prophecy
Kenneth Mackenzie or Coinneach Odhar, generally referred to as the Brahan Seer, is Scotland's most legendary fortune-teller. Some of his predictions read strangely today, written as they are in often rather impenetrable verse. But others are startling in their accuracy.

Mackenzie foretold, amongst other things, the bloody outcome of the Battle of Culloden, the construction of the Caledonian Canal and the Highland Clearances.

Thus he is often hailed as the Gaelic Nostradamus, in reference to the great 17th-century prophet who is claimed to have foretold the rise of Hitler and the Russian Revolution, albeit in cryptic stanzas known as quatrains.

Mackenzie was born on the Isle of Lewis sometime in the early 1600s. Or at least, so the story goes. In fact, there is no actual record of his having existed at all.

There is a Scottish Parliament record, dated 1577, of a Coinneach Odhar, described as an "enchanter", with two writs issued for his arrest. This relates to the case of a Catherine Ross of Balnagowan, married to Robert Mor Munro of Foulis, who had six children by his first marriage and six by his second, to Catherine.

Catherine, it seems, was ambitious for her own children, and hatched a ruthless plan to rid herself of her stepchildren, who stood in the way of their inheritance. She engaged 26 local witches who, the record suggests, were unsuccessful in their endeavour. Coinneach Odhar, whom she engaged subsequently, did a rather better job, providing her with poison.

Alas, the record does not tell us if he was ever caught, though he would most certainly have been burnt alive if he had been, and at a town called Fortrose, because Foulis fell within the jurisdiction of Fortrose Cathedral.

Which is where this real record dovetails to some extent with the Brahan Seer legend, as Kenneth Mackenzie is said to have been burnt alive in a spiked tar barrel in Fortrose, and there is a stone slab by Chanonry Point, near the town, which marks where he allegedly died.

However, the dates are a little awry. This Coinneach Odhar was a little early for our seer, leading some to speculate that the sorcerer was possibly the grandfather of the prophet, his supernatural gifts being put to rather less murderous use a couple of generations on.

However, the two most famous explanations of how Mackenzie gained his gift do not take a family gene pool into account.

The first story has it that Mackenzie's mother was out one

night, tending to her cattle. It was nearing midnight when she approached a local hill called Cnoceothall, which overlooked a burial ground. As the witching hour struck, she saw the graves open up and the dead rise, their ghostly forms drifting away in all directions. An hour later, they all returned, their graves shutting up behind them.

All but one, that is. Mackenzie's mother walked up to this one and placed her staff across it, thereby preventing the spirit from re-entering its resting-place. Shortly afterwards, the ghost of a beautiful woman drifted into the graveyard and, seeing the barrier in her way, begged for it to be removed. Mackenzie's mother, clearly possessed of a typically Highland curiosity, said she would, but only if the ghost first told her why she had returned so much later than the others.

The ghost-woman explained that she had been to Norway, and was in fact the King of Norway's drowned daughter. Following the tragic accident, her body had been borne across the sea, finally washing up on a nearby shore. Hence her burial here in Lewis.

She then promised that, if she was allowed to pass, she would reward her interlocutor with a "valuable secret", instructing Mackenzie's mother to go to a nearby loch and seek out a small, round blue stone which she should then pass on to her son, Kenneth. This, said the ghost, would give him the power to predict the future.

This she did, presumably having let the poor ghost pass, and her son was duly blessed with the gift of second sight. As an adult, Kenneth Mackenzie moved to Brahan, an estate on the mainland near Inverness, where he worked as a labourer, yet told the fortunes of some of the richest families in the land. Which gives us an indication of the strict social order of those days; "upwardly mobile" was not a familiar concept to our 17th century forebears.

The second story, cited by – amongst others – Hugh Miller, resident of nearby Cromarty and known as one of the fathers of geology as well as an enthusiastic and important chronicler of Highland lore, has it that Mackenzie received his gift whilst working on the Brahan estate.

He was cutting peats one day, peats being the primary source of fuel in the Highlands in those days, in a location some distance from his master and mistress's house. It being so far away that he would lose valuable daylight hours returning to the house for dinner, his midday meal was taken out to him by his mistress, who had taken the opportunity to lace the repast with poison.

The background to this story being that Mackenzie had made a nuisance of himself, teasing the mistress to the point where she found him unendurable. However, her plan to poison him was foiled because he fell asleep beforehand and, upon waking, felt something hard pressing on his heart. The source of the pressure was a hard white stone, with a hole in the middle, which had mysteriously appeared in his waistcoat pocket.

Looking through the hole, he had a vision of his mistress lacing his food with poison and was thus forewarned. Just to make sure, when the meal did arrive, he fed it to his faithful hound and watched, in dismay, as the unfortunate creature died in agony in front of him.

The stone is alleged to have left him blind in one eye, but with the other he was to see many incredible things indeed.

Most storytellers agree that the gift of prophecy was bequeathed by the stone but Miller, who was nothing if not a rational man, believed it was more of a gimmick designed to lend Mackenzie gravitas and that the gift, if it existed, was inherent.

"If Kenneth was really possessed of the power of prophecy, he more than likely used the stone simply to impose upon the people, who would never believe him possessed of such a gift unless they saw with their own eyes the means by which he exercised it."

Kenneth Mackenzie made many uncanny predictions, some relating to the future of wealthy families of the area, some to changes that would occur in the local area in years to come, and others reaching far into the future, touching on the Industrial Revolution, the reign of Victoria, even the modern age of oil platforms and aviation.

The Caledonian Canal

Tomnahurich is a large hill sited near the Highland capital of

Inverness. For many centuries it was regarded as a "fairies' hill" into which human beings could be enchanted by fairies, often never to return.

Though it was situated reasonably near a series of inland lochs, it was very much a landlocked hill. So it came as a great surprise when Mackenzie declared:

"Strange as it may seem to you this day, and it is not far off, when full-rigged ships will be seen sailing eastward and westward by the back of Tomnahurich, near Inverness."

Yet it came to pass.

In the early nineteenth century – 1802–1833 – Thomas Telford designed and built the Caledonian Canal, connecting those inland lochs to the sea. It was created to provide safe passage for Royal Navy ships during the Napoleonic War, so there would indeed have been fully-rigged, sea-going vessels seen navigating around Tomnahurich, both eastward and westward.

Strathpeffer Spa

"Uninviting and disagreeable as it is, with its thick-crusted surface and unpleasant smell, the day will come when it shall be under lock and key and crowds...will throng to its portals."

Here Mackenzie was describing the sulphur springs at Strathpeffer, a small Highland town near the Brahan estate. These springs were a source of disgust in the 17th century with their loathsome rotten egg smell.

But reel two centuries forward, and Strathpeffer had become one of the Victorians favourite spas, a place where the afflicted came flocking to "take the waters", believed by then to have great restorative powers.

These days, you can still taste of the waters, and the smart Victorian hotels, railway station and town-houses are testament to how truly Mackenzie's bizarre prediction came true.

The Highland Clearances

In Mackenzie's day, the Highlands and Islands of Scotland were populous places, a patchwork of small subsistence crofts and townships, where generations succeeded generations.

These days, the Highlands are considered Europe's only

wilderness. You can travel for miles in any direction and not encounter a single person. Instead are acres upon acres of empty, untended land, marked with the occasional ruined homestead.

What happened in between times was one of the most terrible crimes against humanity witnessed in Scotland, when thousands were swept off the land they had tended for centuries by landlords grown greedy for profit. Many died, of starvation or being burnt alive in their own homes. Others migrated to the cities, or to the New Worlds in Canada and Australia.

Mackenzie saw it all.

"The day will come, and it is not far off, when farm-steadings will be so few and far between that the cock of a crow shall not be heard from one steading to the other."

He even predicted what would take the place of man – sheep. Though his phraseology is perhaps a little brutal on the poor Highlanders who saw their crops burnt and their wives mistreated before their very eyes.

"The clans will become so effeminate as to flee from their native country before an army of sheep."

Culloden

One of Mackenzie's most famous predictions is that of Culloden. A vision seized him one day, as he was passing Culloden Moor, near Drumossie, on the far side of Inverness.

"Oh! Drummossie, thy bleak moor shall, ere many generations have passed away, be stained with the best blood of the Highlands. Glad am I that I will not see the day, for it will be a frightful period; heads will be lopped off by the score, and no mercy shall be shown or quarter given on either side."

He was not far wrong. Only a century after his passing, in 1746, was the Battle of Culloden, the last to be fought on British soil. The Hanoverians, in the pay of the English king, routed the forces of Bonnie Prince Charlie, comprised mostly of Highlanders.

Because the Jacobites had been such a thorn in the Hanoverian side, the Duke of Cumberland was given strict instructions to show no mercy in victory and he carried those orders out to the letter. Not only were the Highlanders soundly defeated, those left wounded on the battlefield afterwards were butchered where they lay.

So many died that day that bodies were simply identified by clan and tossed into mass graves, the markers of which can be seen to this day.

Piper Alpha and the Lockerbie disaster

Kenneth Mackenzie once predicted that "when the ninth bridge crosses the River Ness, there will be fire, flood and calamity."

And for years, the civic planners of Inverness resisted building a ninth bridge, lest they tempt fate. However, by 1987, it seems that Mackenzie's words were forgotten and construction began on a new bridge across the River Ness.

That year, the oil platform Piper Alpha exploded in the North Sea, killing 187 men. Survivors describe how the platform went up like a ball of flame, and how they could only escape by diving into what looked like a sea of molten fire.

A year later came the calamity, when Pan-Am flight 103 blew up above the small town of Lockerbie, its falling wreckage devastating the town below and adding local residents to the death toll of passengers. In total, 279 people died.

Then came the flood. In 1989, a huge spring rainfall caused dreadful flooding, finally washing away the rail bridge and thus, temporarily at least, returning the River Ness bridge tally to eight.

The tale of the Jaw-bone

"The day will come when the Lewsmen shall go forth with their hosts to battle, but they will be turned back by the jaw-bone of an animal smaller than an ass."

This was one of Mackenzie's most incomprehensible predictions yet it came true, and in a quite remarkable way.

In 1745, information was received by those loyal to Bonnie Prince Charlie that he was about to land in Scotland in a bid to raise an army and once again lead a rebellion.

The Earl of Seaforth had previously been a great supporter of the Young Pretender, an allegience that had temporarily cost him his lands. Having had them recently restored to him, he was advised against being seen to join up with the Jacobite forces again.

However, he had already issued private orders to Stornoway to have his men, the famous Lewsmen, sent in readiness to assist

Charlie. Keen to put the brakes on the venture, he hurried towards the West Coast and saw two ships on the horizon, armed to the teeth with battle-ready Lewsmen.

As it happened, Seaforth had just been dining on a sheep's head, and so he used the jaw-bone to signal to the ships to turn tail at once.

Thus the brave Lewsman were turned back from battle by a jaw-bone of an animal smaller than an ass.

The Curse of the Seaforths

The last, and perhaps most epic, of all the Brahan Seer stories is that relating to the Seaforths, an ancient and landed family whose estates sprawled across the Highlands.

The events occurred shortly after the restoration of King Charles II, when Kenneth, the Third Earl of Seaforth, was summoned to Paris on business, leaving his wife the Countess at home alone at Brahan Castle.

But he tarried and he tarried in the French metropolis and she became anxious, finally calling in the Seer to ascertain whether her husband was safe and well.

Looking through his stone, Mackenzie saw that the Earl was thriving in Paris, thanks to fine wine and even finer women. Chuckling to himself, he assured the Countess that, yes, the Earl was safe and well.

The Countess was not satisfied with this and besides, Mackenzie's smirking manner had raised her heckles. Mackenzie, knowing that what he had seen would only raise her ire still further, bade her be satisfied that her Lord was safe and well and ask no more.

But she insisted, growing increasingly angry with the Seer, who responded reluctantly:

"As you will know that which will make you unhappy, I must tell you the truth.

"My lord seems to have little thought of you, or of his children, or of his Highland home. I saw him in a gay gilded room, grandly decked out in velvets, with silks and cloth of gold, and on his knees before a fair lady, his arm round her waist, and her hand pressed to his lips."

This did not please the Countess, especially as she realised she had made him reveal all in front of the servants. The gentry were notoriously class and status-conscious in those days and there were few things worse than being humiliated in front of your domestic staff.

She determined, therefore, to discredit Mackenzie as this, she hoped, would put paid to any sniggering rumours about her husband's infidelity. How she was going to discredit him we will never know because her ill temper got the better of her and she lashed out with the strongest punishment in her gift...and sentenced the Seer to death.

"You have spoken evil dignities, you have vilified the mighty land; you have defamed a mighty chief in the midst of his vassals, you have abused my hospitality and outraged my feelings, you have sullied the good name of my lord n the halls of his ancestors, and you shall suffer the most signal vengeance I can inflict – you shall suffer death," raged the Countess.

At first, Mackenzie was not unduly alarmed. He assumed she would recover her good spirits and quietly release him. But she never flinched from her vengeful purpose.

He was not allowed to make the case for his defence, nor was there time for anyone of noble standing to intervene on his behalf. The orders were given, and Mackenzie was led out for immediate execution, which took the form of his being burnt alive in a barrel of tar.

Before he went to his doom however, he pulled out his white stone and, looking into the future, declared:

"I see into the far future, and I read the doom of the race of my oppressor.

"The long-descended line of Seaforth will, ere many generations have passed, end in extinction and in sorrow. I see a chief, the last of his house, both deaf and dumb. He will be the father of four fair sons, all of whom he will follow to the tomb. He will live careworn and die mourning, knowing that the honours of his line are to be extinguished for ever, and that no future chief of the Mackenzies shall bear rule at Brahan or in Kintail.

"After lamenting over the last and most promising of his sons, he himself shall sink into the grave, and the remnant of his possessions shall be inherited by a white-coifed (or white-hooded) lassie from the East, and she is to kill her sister.

"And as a sign by which it may be known that these things are coming to pass, there shall be four great lairds in the days of the last deaf and dumb Seaforth – Gairloch, Chisholm, Grant and Raasay – of whom one shall be buck-toothed, another hare-lipped, another half-witted, and the fourth a stammerer. Chiefs distinguished by these personal marks shall be allies and neighbours of the last Seaforth; and when he looks around him and sees them, he may know that his sons are doomed to death, that his broad lands shall pass away to the stranger, and that his race shall come to an end."

It was, by any measure, a fine and dramatic exit and, it seems, came to pass just as he said, but not for over a century.

Indeed, it seemed that the Seer was to be defied as the Seaforths thrived, even surviving – as previously mentioned - the confiscation of their lands following the 1715 Jacobite uprising.

But then, in 1794, was born Francis Humberston Mackenzie, who was to become known as the "last of the Seaforths". He was born with all his faculties intact but following a childhood bout of Scarlet Fever, was left deaf. Though he was still able to speak, he lost that power towards the end of his life.

Nonetheless, he had a successful career in the military, made a good marriage, to Mary Proby, and fathered four sons and six daughters. It was such a good life that he was not alarmed by the fact that four Lairds of his acquaintance, namely Gairloch, Chisholm, Grant and Raasay, had the exact physical peculiarities of which the Kenneth Mackenzie had made mention.

But the prophecy would out. One of Seaforth's sons had died young, and the other three followed him to the grave in time, the last enduring a long illness before finally dying.

Broken-hearted and haunted by the Seer's words, Lord Seaforth followed him to the grave in 1815. Thus the name of Seaforth died out and the lands were indeed inherited by Seaforth's daughter, by then a young widow, often referred to as a "white-hooded lassie", whose married name was Hood.

Upon her second marriage, the Seaforth lands passed into the Earl of Galloway's line, with the Island of Lewis being sold off to a Sir James Matheson.

All of which left only one portion of Kenneth Mackenzie's curse outstanding, that this white-hooded lassie would kill her sister.

This happened some time later. Mrs Stewart Mackenzie as she now was, was driving her young sister Caroline in a horse-drawn carriage through the Brahan estate woods when the horses took fright and bolted, and she lost control.

Both sisters were thrown from the carriage, Mrs Mackenzie recovering at length, but Caroline dying of her injuries.

It was not her fault but because she was the driver of the carriage, the white-hooded lassie could be said to have indeed killed her sister.

So famous is the tale of the Curse of the Seaforths that Sir Walter Scott, the author of the Waverley novels, wrote a poem about it, the Lament for "The Last of the Seaforths".

modern prophets

There have been none since who match Kenneth Mackenzie's fame or uncanny ability to lay his finger on the future. Then again, it has to be remembered that many of the Brahan Seer's predictions took a century of two to play out. So perhaps we will have to wait and see.

However, one seer worthy of mention is Swein MacDonald, who lives in the Highlands, in fact not far from the 17th century home of Mackenzie himself.

MacDonald did not receive his gift in the magical way attributed to the Brahan Seer. Instead, he says, he has always been able to see into the future, a gift passed down through his family, which he can trace back to the 1720s in Sutherland.

His mother had second sight but such was the strength of her Presbyterian faith, she was reluctant to practice it. Her father however, Swein's grandfather, was famous for his ability to predict who would die next. A handy skill given that he worked as a grave-digger.

As a child, MacDonald could see the dead, and even predict occasional, random events, but it was not until much later that he took up this calling seriously.

Though he was born in Elgin, in the North East, MacDonald worked for much of his adult life in Glasgow, as a civil engineer for the Clyde Navigation Trust, before an industrial accident put paid to that. A skip containing a ton of bricks was swinging from a crane when it hit MacDonald, very nearly to his fatal injury.

These days, he walks with a stick and has an impaired sense of both taste and smell. But somehow, this brush with mortality heightened his other senses, notably that relating to prophecy.

He developed tunnel vision, a not uncommon result of severe head injuries, and this in turn seemed to develop what he calls his "third eye", the orifice through which he sees the world to come.

When clients visit him at his home, a small croft overlooking the Dornoch Firth, he ushers them into a consultation room, containing two chairs, which sit facing each other.

Once he and his client are seated, MacDonald offers them pen and paper to take notes if they so wish. Then, without preamble, he begins to talk and many have been astounded by the accuracy with which he describes their lives, family and circumstances.

He then ventures on to the future, offering advice and an insight into critical events to come, finally inviting his sitter to ask him any questions.

The future, he says, reels before him like images in a film but, though he is happy to see anyone and try to help them, he has one hard and fast rule: he will not deliver a bad fortune. If he looks into someone's future and sees only darkness, he will tell them nothing. As many mediums and psychics also say, the future cannot be changed and knowing an ill fate will do nobody any good.

One example of his withholding of evidence, as it were, is cited in Roddy Martine's *Supernatural Scotland*.

Two women had travelled all the way up from Glasgow to see the Dornoch Seer so the second was very disappointed when he told her that he was now exhausted and could not therefore also give her a reading. Despite her earnest pleading, he continued to beg off, citing tiredness. However, when she began to cry with frustration, he relented, saying he would not give her a reading exactly, instead writing down a prophecy on a piece of paper, then sealing it in an envelope. Her part of the bargain was that she must promise not to read it till she got home to Glasgow. This she agreed to, and the two women left, somewhat mollified.

The second woman, who was the driver, slid the sealed prophecy into her handbag before they drove off. On the way home, the car was involved in a horrendous, head-on collision that killed the driver outright, though the passenger survived.

A long time later, this first woman was going through her friend's handbag, just part of the traditional clearing out of a dead person's effects, and chanced upon the sealed prophecy. Under the tragic circumstances, it is no wonder she had forgotten it until now.

Opening it, she found herself staring, not at a prophecy, but at a blank sheet of paper. MacDonald had seen the woman's death and could not bring himself to tell her.

Another time, he forebore to tell a young woman that her parents were soon to die in a car accident. She returned to see him some time later and asked why he had failed to warn her. He responded that he could not tell her something that she could not bear to know, given that she could do nothing to prevent it.

Though MacDonald offers advice on the future, he is firm in his belief that destiny cannot be altered once it is set in motion.

MacDonald has been involved in police work, specifically in tracking down missing persons. In one case, he was asked by an anxious couple in Lanarkshire if he could pinpoint the whereabouts of their runaway son.

Through his third eye, MacDonald saw the young man surrounded by "tall buildings" and knew that he was perfectly safe and would return soon. The only problem he had was a sore shoulder.

As predicted, the son did turn up, complete with sore shoulder. He had been in Castlemilk, a housing scheme in Glasgow, famous for its high-rises.

MacDonald was also consulted by the police when they ran out of leads in the Renee MacRae disappearance of 1976. Renee and her young son had apparently left Inverness one evening but the only trace that has ever been found of them is a burnt-out car in a layby on the A9, the main motorway from Inverness to the South. So far, the case remains a mystery.

Another story involves the discovery of a body in the Cairngorm mountains, near Aviemore. A young man had been reported missing in Inverness and his description matched that of the dead man. His distraught father came to identify the body and, through confirming that it was his son, enabled the police to close the case.

However, a woman in London had recently sought out MacDonald's assistance in tracking down her missing son. She sent him a photograph and, the minute it was in his hands, the seer had a vision of a young man lying dead in a mountain landscape. He had died of hypothermia, a likely enough death in such harsh conditions, but the telling details were that one of his boots was missing and one of his trouser pockets contained a Swiss Army knife.

MacDonald says that when he divines where a missing person is "you get this strange, strange feeling about it. Just once. If anybody is living, it's a good feeling. If somebody is dead, it's a bad feeling. You get this feeling of tension."

Swein phoned the police and convinced them, just through the sheer detail of his description, that the Cairngorms case needed further investigation.

The body was exhumed and a photograph taken was identified by the London woman as indeed that of her son.

Meanwhile, the now quite overwhelmed father learnt that his son had not perished on the hillsides but been on a week-long drinking bender in Inverness.

CURSES

The Brahan Seer was not alone in his ability to deliver curses that appeared to come true. Many insist that curses, because they become embedded in the minds of the cursed, operate simply as self-fulfilling prophecies. The following stories perhaps shed a little doubt on that comforting theory..

Bonnie Dundee – ominous sights

Two stories have been told about the death of John Graham of Claverhouse, Viscount Dundee, 'Bonnie Dundee', the persecutor of the Covenanters who was killed at the Battle of Killiecrankie, a landmark in Scottish history.

The night before the battle, it is said, as Graham slept, he was disturbed by two things. First, he saw a strange red glow in the darkness, which could not be explained by human activity. This same glow has been reportedly seen by visitors to the site on the anniversary of the battle in years since. Ghostly lights are quite a common phenomenon, as has already been mentioned, both as signs of approaching death (death candles) and as spectral 'markers' of places where bloodshed and death have occurred.

The second thing to trouble Graham happened towards the hours of dawn, we are told. He saw a vision of a man by his bed, blood dripping from a head wound. The terrible figure pointed at Graham and cried:

'Remember Brown of Priesthill!'

Brown of Priesthill was a man called John Brown, a Covenanter who was killed for his beliefs. It is said that when the men in the firing squad saw Brown's steadfast courage and unfailing religious conviction in the face of imminent execution, they faltered, and Viscount Dundee himself fired the fatal shot.

Graham was greatly disturbed by the spectre of Brown of Priesthill. Thinking (hoping) that what he had seen had not been a ghost but instead some devious trick by his enemies, he got up and inquired of the sentry whether there had been intruders in the camp. The guard outside, however, said that all had been quiet and that nobody had approached Graham's tent.

The figure that Bonnie Dundee had seen had been a sign – its appearance, along with the eerie red glow, foretold his death in battle the next day.

Another person, many miles away, had a vision to tell him of John Graham's death. He was Lord Balcarres of Colinsburgh, unable to join his acquaintance in battle because he was under arrest on the orders of parliament. On the night after the battle, he was roused from sleep by a sound by his bed. He looked up and saw his comrade, Viscount Dundee, standing by the bed. He rose to greet him but the figure turned away and then disappeared. It was only later that Lord Balcarres found out that Viscount Dundee had been killed in battle that very day.

Sir Walter Scott

Sir Walter Scott had a keen interest in the supernatural, and during his lifetime he witnessed a ghost in his own home. A man from London, called George Bullock, was appointed by Scott to take charge of many of the building works at the writer's home, Abbotsford. George Bullock died in London in 1818, while work was still in progress at Abbotsford, fourteen years before the author's own death.

On the night of Bullock's death, Scott told of being woken by violent noises in the house. Although it was the middle of the night, it sounded as if builders were at work. Scott got up to investigate, but as he made his way through the house apprehensively, sword in hand, he could find nothing to explain the disturbance. The house was quiet again, and there were no signs of any disturbance.

Later, Scott was to discover that the bizarre events coincided with Bullock's death in London. The ghost of Bullock is said to have put in an appearance at Abbotsford on a number of occasions since then.

Visions of the dead in Galloway

Two stories that originate from Galloway in southwest Scotland echo the story of Mr Swan (*see* A Haunted Capital – Ann Street).

The first story concerns an old man, a smallholder, who was working out in the fields on the hillside one afternoon when he caught sight of his son below him in the distance, heading towards their home. The old man called down to his son, but obviously the lad was too far away to hear him.

The old man was consumed with curiosity. His son was a sailor, and the old man was sure that he was supposed to be on a long voyage, still at sea for some weeks to come. All the same, the old man had work to attend to. The potato crop had to be brought in. He hurried on with his task – the sooner he finished, the sooner he would be able to go home and see his son.

The old man had finished his work by lunch time. He hurried back to the cottage to greet his son and hear all his news. But when he got home, there was no sign of the lad. The old man's wife was preparing a meal for two people, just as usual. The old man asked whether their son had been home, but his wife said no.

The old man decided that his eyes had been deceiving him – he had, after all, been high up on the hillside. What he thought had been the figure of his son was probably just a passer-by with a similar appearance.

Some time later, however, the old man and his wife received the tragic news that their son had been killed overseas in an accident – at the time at which his father had thought he had seen him.

The second story concerns a boy who was staying with his grandparents for the summer. The boy was sitting outside in the yard one afternoon, whittling some wood, when he saw his grandfather come out of the house. The old man paused to watch the boy for a few moments, then, without saying a word, walked off out of the yard towards the fields. The boy remarked to himself that the old man seemed uncharacteristically quiet, but he was too absorbed in what he was doing to give the matter much thought.

A few minutes later the boy went back into the house. He was quite taken aback when he saw that his grandfather was there, sitting in his favourite chair by the fire. Hadn't he just seen the old man walk away from the house, dressed in exactly the same clothes? It was the strangest thing – after all, the old man could not be in two places at the same time. Had the boy been dreaming or had his eyes been deceiving him?

Quite unexpectedly, the old man fell ill that night and very shortly afterwards he died. The boy now understood that when he had seen the figure of his grandfather walking away he had been forewarned of the old man's departure to another life.

The cursed mill

Many years ago, near Newtonmore, there was once a mill that was said to be cursed. The curse had been placed on the mill, it was said, by an old witch who had a grievance with the man who owned the mill at that time.

The curse wreaked havoc for some years after that. The first miller was killed in a fire. His successor died of a sudden and mysterious illness, after which the mill was burned to the ground. When the mill was rebuilt, the witch's heart softened a little and she weakened the curse. Now the mill would be safe from further problems as long as it was left idle for one day every year. Woe betide the miller who dared to use the mill on the forbidden day.

Many years later, the mill was bought by an ambitious miller who wanted to expand his business. He already owned one mill and wanted to improve his prospects with the purchase of a second one. He did not hold with superstition, nor did he like the mill at Newtonmore standing idle when he could be making money from it. The so-called witch was long dead, and the miller could not see what harm she could do from the grave.

In spite of warnings not to do so, the miller prepared to keep the mill working on the forbidden day. Hardly had he set the machinery in motion than there was a terrible grating sound and everything came to a halt. The small amount of meal that had been ground was full of grit, and one of the grinding stones had, incredibly, broken into several fragments.

Unwilling to admit that he might have been wrong, the miller denied to all and sundry that he had had any problems. He quietly arranged delivery of a new grinding stone and carried on working for another year.

The next year the miller was still determined to keep the mill working on the forbidden day. But this time not one piece of machinery would function in spite of the most careful maintenance. Nothing seemed to be wrong, but, all the same, nothing would work. To add to his grief and frustration, the miller discovered that a sudden and voracious plague of rats in his granary had eaten all his corn.

The miller had experienced quite enough. He sold the mill, deciding it was better to concentrate all his efforts on the other mill that he owned. His troubles were not over, however. His first mill was destroyed by fire, and he himself took ill and died very soon afterwards.

The cursed mill was then taken over by yet another man, a kindly and earnest soul who had taken a young gypsy boy under his wing. They managed to set the mill to rights, and it worked beautifully, making them a good living until the old man died. The gypsy boy left to find a job elsewhere, and another miller stepped in to run the mill. Although the machinery had been well maintained and everything appeared to be in good working order, the mill refused to work properly and the miller was plagued with problems. The gypsy boy was summoned to give his advice, and much to everyone's amazement, with a tweak here and a twiddle there, he managed to get the mill to work. Nobody could work out how he did it. And yet, no sooner had he left the premises than the mill ground to a halt yet again. The miller threw up his hands in despair and left.

The gypsy boy returned to the mill to take charge. As long as he was there, the mill worked perfectly well and he made himself a good living. But after his death the mill fell into disrepair. Because of the angry words of an old woman, long dead, nobody else could ever get it to work again.

The curse of Alloa Tower

Alloa Tower stands bleakly empty nowadays, a haven for rodents and nesting birds and a magnet for vandals who have left their handiwork on the boards that cover up the doors and windows. The dereliction of the place adds to the air of grimness that surrounds it, but its proud tall walls and castellated turrets remain intact, as if making one last determined stand against the curse on the Erskines, Earls of Mar, the family who once owned it.

Exactly when the terrible curse was first uttered is uncertain; some sources believe it to date from the sixteenth century. At that time the Abbey of Cambuskenneth was destroyed by the Earl of Mar, and some people believe that it was the abbot who pronounced the curse upon the family. When it was pronounced and by whom do not matter so much as the horrifying manner in which events followed to bring about the demise of the Erskines, exactly as the curse had promised.

The curse promised the following things:

- The family would become extinct.
- The estates of the Erskine family would fall into the hands of strangers.
- One of the Erskines would live to see his home, a place where a king was raised, ravaged by flames. He would see his wife die in the burning house.
- Three of that man's children would never see the light of day.
- The great hall of his house would become a place for stabling horses.

BiBLiOgRapHy

RefeReNCes aNb fuRtHeR Reabing

Hellish Nell: Last of Britain's Witches by Malcolm Gaskill (Fourth Estate, 2001)

Not of this World by Maurice Fleming (Mercat Press, 2002)

The Unbelievable Truth by Gordon Smith (Hay House, 2004)

Spirit Messenger by Gordon Smith (Hay House, 2003)

'Best' of Both Worlds by Rosalind Cattanach (Pembridge Publishing, 1999)

A Sense of Something Strange by Archie E Roy (Dog and Bone, 1990)

Supernatural Scotland by Roddy Martine (Robert Hale, 2003)

Ley Lines and Earth Energies by David R Cowan (David Hatcher Childress, California, 2004)

News souRCes

Sunday Herald (5 May 2001: Theatre call in exorcist to halt ghostly encore, by James Hamilton; 16 March 2003: The Exorcist Files by Vicky Allan)

The Guardian (2 May 2001: Exorcism: abuse or curse? by David Batty)

Christiantoday.com: (19 December 2004: Deliverance Group Recommends the Church of Scotland a Cautious Approach to Exorcism)

Haunted Scotland Journal (various dates, ed: Mark Fraser)

Other titles available
from **LOMOND BOOKS**:

Scottish Witches & Wizards

Scottish Murders

Scottish Ghosts

Scottish Myths & Legends

Scottish Jokes

Scottish Songs

Traditional Scottish Cookery